ROUTLEDGE LIBRARY EDITIONS: THE VICTORIAN WORLD

Volume 1

THREE VICTORIAN TRAVELLERS

THREE VICTORIAN TRAVELLERS
Burton, Blunt, Doughty

THOMAS J. ASSAD

Routledge
Taylor & Francis Group
LONDON AND NEW YORK

First published in 1964 by Routledge and Kegan Paul Ltd

This edition first published in 2016
by Routledge
2 Park Square, Milton Park, Abingdon, Oxon OX14 4RN

and by Routledge
711 Third Avenue, New York, NY 10017

Routledge is an imprint of the Taylor & Francis Group, an informa business

© 1964 Thomas J. Assad

All rights reserved. No part of this book may be reprinted or reproduced or utilised in any form or by any electronic, mechanical, or other means, now known or hereafter invented, including photocopying and recording, or in any information storage or retrieval system, without permission in writing from the publishers.

Trademark notice: Product or corporate names may be trademarks or registered trademarks, and are used only for identification and explanation without intent to infringe.

British Library Cataloguing in Publication Data
A catalogue record for this book is available from the British Library

ISBN: 978-1-138-66565-1 (Set)
ISBN: 978-1-315-61965-1 (Set) (ebk)
ISBN: 978-1-138-63842-6 (Volume 1) (hbk)
ISBN: 978-1-138-63844-0 (Volume 1) (pbk)
ISBN: 978-1-315-63780-8 (Volume 1) (ebk)

Publisher's Note
The publisher has gone to great lengths to ensure the quality of this reprint but points out that some imperfections in the original copies may be apparent.

Disclaimer
The publisher has made every effort to trace copyright holders and would welcome correspondence from those they have been unable to trace.

THREE VICTORIAN TRAVELLERS

BURTON, BLUNT
DOUGHTY

by
THOMAS J. ASSAD

ROUTLEDGE & KEGAN PAUL
LONDON

*First published 1964
by Routledge and Kegan Paul Ltd
Broadway House, 68–74 Carter Lane
London, E.C.4*

*Printed in Great Britain
by Butler and Tanner Ltd
Frome and London*

Copyright Thomas J. Assad 1964

*No part of this book may be reproduced
in any form without permission from
the Publisher, except for the quotation
of brief passages in criticism*

Contents

PREFACE	*page* ix
I. VICTORIAN INTEREST IN THE ARAB WORLD	1
II. RICHARD FRANCIS BURTON—HAJI	9
III. WILFRID SCAWEN BLUNT—SHEIKH	53
IV. CHARLES MONTAGU DOUGHTY—NASRÂNY	95
V. DOUGHTY, BLUNT, AND BURTON	133
NOTES	138
INDEX	151

Illustrations

(*Between pages 134 and 135*)

1. Burton as a young man
(From *The National Portrait Gallery*, vol. 2, page 252, London, 1902)

2. Burton in desert robes
(From *Harper's Magazine*, vol. 14, page 180, January 1857)

3. Burton as an old man
(From Stisted, G., *The True Life of Captain Sir Richard F. Burton*, Frontispiece, London, 1896)

4. Mr and Lady Blunt
(From *Illustrated London News*, vol. 92, Mr. 3, page 223, 1888)

5. Blunt in desert robes
(From Blunt, Lady Anne, *A Pilgrimage to Nejd*, Frontispiece, Murray, London, 1881)

6. Blunt in a turban
(From *The Bookbuyer*, vol. 12, no. 10, page 559, November 1895)

7. Doughty as a young man
(From *The Bookman*, vol. 72, page 161, June 1927)

8. Doughty as an old man
(From *The Bookman*, vol. 69, page 289, March 1926)

Preface

THIS book is concerned with impressions of Arabic culture on British sensibilities before the first World War. More particularly, it is concerned with three Victorian travellers, all of whom knew Arabic culture at first hand through their travels in the Middle or Near East, and especially in Arabia, Arabic North Africa, and the seaboard of the eastern Mediterranean. The present atmosphere, made heavy with partisan zeal and clouded by the powerful instruments of modern propaganda, is not conducive to clear perception; but when we step through this period to a time some thirty or forty years before that war, the passion of the present is swept away and we can see as in the detached, broad outlines of history the fundamental British attitudes towards the Arabs.

These attitudes are most clearly discernible in the informed, widely circulated opinions of British men of letters who had intimate contacts with the Arabs. It is unfortunate in this respect that the career of T. E. Lawrence has overshadowed the importance of his English predecessors in the Arab world. His daring exploits during the war of 1914–18 and the subsequent popularity of *The Seven Pillars of Wisdom* enabled him to capture the imagination of the English-speaking public in the early twentieth century. And yet his remarkable expeditions in the East, his adhibition of Arabic culture, and his political intentions—whatever may be the final estimate of these—were anticipated by Sir Richard Francis Burton, Wilfrid Scawen Blunt, and Charles Montagu Doughty. And taken together, the views of Burton, Blunt, and Doughty are fairly representative of the late-Victorian attitudes towards the Arab world. Although Burton was born some twenty years before the others and his best travel-books were published in the 'fifties, the most important

Preface

decade for this study is the 'eighties, when Burton was working on his translation of the *Arabian Nights*, Blunt was deeply immersed in Eastern politics, and Doughty was laboriously writing *Arabia Deserta*. And this is precisely the time when British Imperialism reached its peak.

With their palpably different sentiments regarding British Imperialism, and with their no less palpably different temperaments, Burton, Blunt, and Doughty came to three different views, each of which was thought to be the proper understanding of the Arab world. It is all too easy for us to point out the limitations of these views: Burton's view of the Arab was too grotesque; Blunt's, too ornate, too sentimental; and Doughty's, too pure, too simple, too harsh. In each instance, the particular view joined with an innate feeling that the Englishman was *ipso facto* superior to the Arab and therefore engendered the respective modes of mastery, condescension, and chauvinism. It is much more difficult to understand the temperaments and sensibilities which made these views so colourful; but the attempt is extremely rewarding in that it involves three fascinating men in an extremely lively period of human history.

In attempting to approach an understanding of these authors —an understanding of their sensibilities and the effect of the impact of Arabic culture on those sensibilities—I have given primary attention to a consideration of such of their writings as deal directly with the Middle East. But frequently, and especially with Blunt, whose prose is predominantly autobiographical and political in nature, I have emphasized extra-Eastern material. I believe that in such instances the chapter as a whole will vindicate the relevance of what by themselves may appear to be unimportant digressions.

T. J. A.

I
Victorian Interest in the Arab World

WHEN Cardinal Newman in his *Apologia Pro Vita Sua* wanted to impress upon his readers his powers of imagination as a boy, he chose to relate his experience with the *Arabian Nights* as a good illustration. He wrote, 'I used to wish the Arabian Tales were true: my imagination ran on unknown influences, on magical powers, and talismans.' In *Sartor Resartus* Carlyle explained the Professor's attitude towards miracles by having him say, 'To my horse, again, who unhappily is still more unscientific [than the "Dutch King of Siam"], do not I work a miracle, a magical "Open sesame!" every time I please to pay twopence, and open for him an impossible *Schlagbaum*, or shut Turnpike?' And Ruskin in *Sesame and Lilies* used the same allusion to Ali Baba when he exhorted his audience to favour the propagation of books and libraries, to get new corn laws established for the 'British constitution'—corn laws 'dealing in a better bread;—bread made up of that old enchanted Arabian grain, the Sesame, which opens doors;—doors not of robbers', but of Kings' Treasuries'.

It would be very difficult to find many Victorian writers who did not make some allusion to Eastern literature,[1] and most frequent are the references such as these to the *Arabian Nights*, used primarily in similes and metaphors for the purpose of illustration. Although a comprehensive survey of such allusions would be as impracticable as an investigation of Biblical references in the same literature, the few examples above, because of the very nature of these figures of speech, clearly indicate that at least certain tales of the *Arabian Nights* had become common knowledge, not only to the more important writers and thinkers of the period, but to the general reading public as well.

English readers throughout the eighteenth century knew the *Arabian Nights* only through anglicized versions and adaptations of Antoine Galland's selective and very freely rendered French translation of 1704. It was not until nearly a century later that the orientalist Dr. Jonathan Scott used Eastern sources directly in his *Tales, Anecdotes, and Letters from the Arabic and Persian* (1800), followed in 1811 by *The Arabian Nights' Entertainment*. Scott's translation became the source of many English versions of the *Nights* and was itself reprinted in 1883. Meanwhile, other translators were at work. In 1838 an Irish lawyer, Henry Torrens, began an accurate translation of the *Nights* but produced in all only one volume of tales. Edward William Lane's *New Translation of the Tales of a Thousand Nights and One Night* appeared in 1839 and went through four editions. This translation contained only a small portion of the complete Arabic tales and some of the shorter tales appeared merely as notes; but these latter were given more currency in 1845 when they were published separately as *Arabian Tales and Anecdotes* and in 1883 when Stanley Lane-Poole published a classified and arranged edition of Lane's notes under the title *Arabian Society in the Middle Ages*. John Payne's translation, *The Book of The Thousand Nights and One Night* (1882–4), was the first complete translation of the *Nights*, but it was limited to five hundred copies. Richard F. Burton's complete and literal translation was privately printed for subscribers only (1885–8) and was limited to one thousand copies.

Scholarly works on the East and translations of Eastern literature other than the *Arabian Nights* also multiplied during the latter part of the nineteenth century. For the most part, even the translations were the work of reputable Arabists. Between the publication of William Wright's *The Travels of Ibn Jubair* in 1852 and Sir Charles James Lyall's *Two Ancient Arabic Diwans; with Translation* in 1913, there is a very impressive bibliography of English scholarship in Arabic language and literature.[2] The result was the growth of a more accurate awareness of Eastern culture, an awareness which coincided with a more earnest political interest in the Middle East.

Victorian Interest in the Arab World

England and France had supported Turkey in the Crimean war in the belief that Turkey could control her Empire and live in harmony with the European powers.[3] Thus Russia's threatening position with respect to India was made less ominous. But some twenty years later, when the Christian Serbs and Bulgarians revolted against Turkish rule in 1876, Russia saw her opportunity to move again. This presented a difficult problem for England; for in the uprising and its aftermath some Christians had been massacred. Gladstone aroused English public opinion against the 'unspeakable Turk' and advocated ousting the Turks from Europe, 'bag and baggage'. Propaganda, of course, centred about the poor Christians who had been killed. On the other hand, Disraeli, concerned with Russia's new threat to India, supported the Turks. In 1875 Disraeli had adroitly managed to gain for England an interest in the Suez Canal by using Rothschild money to pay the Egyptian Khedive's debts in return for Egypt's shares in the Suez Canal enterprise. Having secured this control over a vital crossroad between England and her Eastern possessions, Disraeli now, at the Congress of Berlin (June 13 to July 13, 1878), was anxious to have British influence extend to Asiatic Turkish possessions so that there would be considerable British control of the route to India from the Mediterranean through Middle Asia and the Persian Gulf. Thus by secret agreement he gained for England the occupation and administration of Cyprus and granted, as a concession to France, England's consent to French seizure of Tunis, which was carried out in 1881.

In this same year, 1881, the Egyptian army revolted under one of its colonels, Arabi Pasha. The revolt was perhaps part of an Egyptian nationalist movement which opposed Turkish rule and domination by European creditors. Fifty Europeans were massacred by mobs in the revolt, and England under Gladstone stepped in to save the Egyptian government. In July, 1882, Alexandria was bombarded and in September Sir Garnet Wolseley destroyed Arabi's army by overwhelming his desert camp at Tel-el-Kebir. In 1883 Gladstone sent Evelyn Baring (later Lord Cromer) to Egypt as British Agent and Consul-General, a post which he held until his resignation in 1907. Technically, Cromer offered 'advice' to the Khedive; but because the Egyptian government's sole protection was English support, and because British troops were stationed in Egypt as 'guests', Cromer's words of advice became virtual commands. Cromer was thus the supreme authority in Egypt and he set about the task of reform. His policy was designed to stabilize the financial condition of the country, and he put into effect measures of strict economy and continued the burdensome taxation of the peasants. He also urged the withdrawal of Egyptian troops from the Sudan, where they were carrying on an unsuccessful and costly campaign against the Mahdi. General Gordon was dispatched from England to effect this withdrawal, but the operation was delayed to the extent that Gordon was trapped and murdered by fanatical mobs at Khartoum in January, 1885. A measure of the British public's attention to the Middle East was the fact that Gladstone never recovered the loss of political prestige which resulted from this disaster. But in 1896 Sir Herbert Kitchener, Sidar of the Egyptian army, began operations against the Sudan and in 1898 his superior weapons annihilated the Mahdi's army at Omdurman outside Khartoum. The Sudan fell unconditionally to British and Egyptian rule and Gordon was considered avenged.[4]

Since Lytton Strachey, one can hardly think of Gordon without visualizing the Bible under his arm and the missionary gleam in his eye. And indeed English missionary spirit turned its attention to the East with increasing intensity in the latter part of the nineteenth century. In 1937 the Near East Council meeting in Alexandria resolved in part: '... we the members of this council purpose to pursue in the years immediately before us a fearless and extensive study of the causes of the comparatively small success in the effort to win Moslems to Christ and to strive with all our strength with God's help to discover the winning way to the heart of the Moslem peoples.'[5] But the lack of success came about through no lack of effort. The modern Protestant missionary movement got under way shortly before the beginning of the nineteenth century and from the very outset efforts were made to reach Moslems in the Middle East. The first board to undertake this work was the Church Missionary Society through its 'Mediterranean Mission' which operated from 1815 to 1850 with headquarters usually at Malta. The Presbyterians of Scotland and Ireland began their missionary work in Damascus in 1843. The London Society for Promoting Missions among the Jews began work in Palestine as early as 1826, but the first substantial fruits of their labours—the first Protestant Church in the Turkish Empire, a training institution for converted Jews, and a hospital—came between 1843 and 1849. Protestant missionary work in Egypt was carried on by Anglicans and United Presbyterians who first sent missionaries through the country on their way to Abyssinia. In 1861 the Church Missionary Society began missionary work in Egypt. It worked in the vicinity of Aden on the Arabian peninsula beginning in 1886 with Keith-Falconer who died in the following year.

The motives of travellers in the second half of the nineteenth century were varied: missionary zeal, the love of adventure, the quest for romance, and scientific inquiry sent the Victorians all over the globe. Accounts of these travels in the Middle East range from archaeological reports such as Sir Austin Henry Layard's *Discoveries at Nineveh* (1851) to the boisterous narratives of Richard Burton. Alexander William Kinglake humorously discussed his travels in the East in *Eothen* (1844); Eliot Warburton's *The Crescent and Cross* (1844) is somewhat more ambitious but less striking; and Robert Curzon's *Monasteries of the Levant* (1849) is an account of the author's search for ancient manuscripts. The *Journal of the Discovery of the Source of the Nile* was published in 1863 by John Henning Speke, who travelled with Burton into central Africa and separated from Burton to make one of the great geographical discoveries of the century. William Gifford Palgrave (brother of the anthologist Francis Turner Palgrave) was a very colourful and controversial figure. Of Jewish ancestry, he became a Jesuit, travelled in Arabia perhaps on a secret mission for France, and left the Jesuits when he published his *Narrative of a Year's Journey through Central and Eastern Arabia* in 1865. Later narratives of experiences in the Middle East are *A Year among the Persians* (1893) by Edward G. Browne, *Persian Pictures* (1894) and *The Desert and the Sown* (1907) by Gertrude Bell, and *A Wandering Scholar in the Levant* (1896) and *Accidents of an Antiquary's Life* (1910) by David G. Hogarth.

Travel, religion, and politics combine in a unique way in the life of Laurence Oliphant (1829–88).[6] We must pass over the most dramatic parts of his life: his early success in the worldly world; his triumphs in politics; his very popular satire, *Piccadilly*; his renunciation of the world and the brilliant career it was promising him; his abject subservience to Thomas Lake Harris as a worker in the 'uses' of the Brotherhood of the New Life in western New York; and his growth, together with that of his wife Alice Le Strange, as a prophet in a sexual mysticism involving a theory of 'counterpartal marriage'.

Oliphant explained his interest in the East in a letter dated December 10, 1878:

> My Eastern project is as follows: To obtain a concession from the Turkish Government in the northern and more fertile half of Palestine, which the recent survey of the Palestine Exploration Fund proves to be capable of immense development. Any amount of money can be raised upon it, owing to the belief which people have that they would be fulfilling prophecy and bringing on the end of the world. I don't know why they are anxious for this latter event, but it makes the commercial speculation easy, as it is a combination of the financial and sentimental elements which will, I think, ensure success. And it will be a good political move for the Government, as it will enable them to carry out reforms in Asiatic Turkey, provide money for the Porte, and by uniting the French in it, and possibly the Italians, be a powerful religious move against the Russians, who are trying to obtain a hold of the country by their pilgrims. It would also secure the Government a large religious support in this country, as even the Radicals would waive their political in favour of their religious crotchets.[7]

He left England in the Spring of 1879 and went directly to Beirut. He travelled about the area seeking a site for his colony and described his expedition in *The Land of Gilead* which was designed also to promote his scheme. There was immediate enthusiastic response from the Jews in Roumania and other persecuted districts. Back in England in 1880 he was reunited with his wife who had been in California with the Harris group and they immediately made plans for a journey to Egypt. The record of this journey appeared in *The Land of Khemi*. In the summer of 1881 Oliphant visited California, formally broke

Victorian Interest in the Arab World

with Harris, and was successful in regaining the property which he had bought in Brocton, New York, and which he had turned over to Harris. His wife meanwhile received a telegram from the United States asking for her authority to have her husband committed to a madhouse, proceedings to that end having already been started. Early in 1882 Oliphant returned to England to find that his wife had broken Harris' strong hold over her and had sided with her husband. In the same year the Oliphants occupied themselves with the plan for Jewish colonization in Palestine and when the plan fell through they took up residence in Haifa.

Oliphant invited his friends at Brocton to join him at Haifa and his residence became a Utopian colony devoted to the practice of a mystical conception of sexual love as the way of the true life. It is equally difficult to believe or to discredit the charges of immorality which were hurled at the Oliphants. Perhaps we will never know whether or not Alice indeed slept with the Arabs in order to bring about a union of the individual with his spiritual counterpart, as Hanah Whitall Smith charged, or whether Oliphant himself, co-administrator of this new way of life, considered and practised such acts as consummations of the scheme's mystical rites.[8] But we do know that the Vigilance Association at London had received complaints, and that litigation was threatened and then dropped at Oliphant's death.[9]

But as his biographer has written, 'these are mysteries with which only a mind entirely in sympathy should attempt to meddle'. In any case, Oliphant's influence on the Arab world seems to have been slight. Mrs. Margaret Oliphant Oliphant reported that only one Arab was converted to Oliphant's doctrines, and this in spite of the great pains Oliphant took in having his doctrines translated into Arabic and Hebrew and supported by quotations from the Koran and the Old Testament. Believing that all religions contained in a hidden manner the system of counterparts which he espoused, he also had intentions of presenting his doctrines to the Hindus and the Buddhists with many quotations from their religious books and traditions.

Oliphant had some superficial contacts with Richard Burton, Wilfrid Blunt, and Charles Doughty. Isabel Burton wrote that

Oliphant had persuaded Captain Speke to anticipate Burton's report on the exploration of the sources of the Nile, and that this report to the Royal Geographical Society was the cause of a bitter dispute between Burton and Speke. She also wrote that when she confronted Oliphant with the charge, he begged her forgiveness for his rash act and could not explain the reasons for his provoking the bitter enmity.[10] Oliphant also talked to Blunt about his scheme for colonization in Palestine and impressed Blunt with his good looks.[11] And he magnanimously offered to rewrite *Arabia Deserta* for Doughty so that it would be acceptable to a publisher.[12] Oliphant's slight acquaintance with the East, while it seems to contain in it his age's general religious and political interests in the Arab world, is yet unique; and unlike the experiences of Burton, Blunt, and Doughty, that acquaintance made no lasting or recurring impression on his sensibilities.

II

Richard Francis Burton—Haji

I

RICHARD FRANCIS BURTON is most spectacularly recorded in history as the traveller-explorer extraordinary, and his place in literature depends in large measure upon the volumes he himself wrote narrating his travels and adventures. While his travel-books are in themselves impressive enough, they have a further significance in unmistakably testifying to a dauntless courage, a personal heroism, and a love for adventure sufficiently outstanding to distinguish the author from the other remarkable travellers and explorers of the nineteenth century.

Fairfax Downey dates Burton's travels from the age of three when the boy's family began searching throughout the Continent for a dry climate where the elder Burton's suffering from asthma might be relieved. The 'nomad caravan' never stayed long at one place, 'a ship always waiting at the dock, their yellow coach at the door. So was bred an explorer. So was the wanderer's curse early fulfilled.'[1] Of course Downey is romanticizing the life of Burton by snatching up insinuations of exotic ancestry, the alluring bait held out by Isabel Burton in her 'consecrated' *Life* of her husband.[2] But whether or not we are interested in hinting that Burton's veins carried that precious drop of gypsy or Arab blood, we must admit that the early wanderings of the Burton family are indeed significant in an analysis of the writer's sensibility. It is impossible at this late date to achieve through psychoanalysis an accurate and profitable evaluation of the effect of Burton's early environment upon his life; but no scientific corroboration is necessary to establish the fact that the circumstance of Continental experience at such an early age helped to make Burton a man apart from the typical nineteenth-century Englishman. Burton himself was regretfully aware of it when he wrote of his college days, apologizing for his academic and social incompatibility and attributing it to his lack of English preparatory school training and to his being dragged 'about the Continent, under governesses and tutors, to learn fencing, languages, and become wild, and to belong to nowhere in particular as to parish or county'. This whole period of school and college he looked back upon as a horrible nightmare: 'It was like the "Blackingshop" of Charles Dickens,' wrote Burton in 1876. But the reader of his journals would never make the comparison. Burton relates incident after incident of boyish deviltry ranging from the breaking of a pastry-shop window in France (when Burton's mother attempted to give the children a lesson in self denial by letting them look but not have) to the instigation of a riot at a brothel in Italy. It is no wonder that he found Oxford life dull and monotonous.

And yet the monotony seems to have been quite often broken, for Burton's journals as quoted by his wife allude to a variety of extracurricular activities and interests—more than enough to keep an ordinary young man from becoming bored with three terms of academic life. But it is the variety, or rather the range of these activities and interests which is important in forming an estimate of Burton's sensibility. At one extreme we note his interest and participation in drinking bouts and boxing. He describes briefly the disapproval of Mrs. Grundy of his foreign ways and his 'expressed dislike to school and college', over which he 'ought to have waxed sentimental, tender, and aesthetic', and he juxtaposes a strong hint that he enjoyed visiting his friends at Brasenose, 'then famous for drinking heavy beers and ales . . . especially on Shrove Tuesday, when certain verses chaffingly called "Carmen seculare" used to be sung'. But he was even more delighted with Oriel where he associated with a small group of students who were interested in boxing and took lessons from 'Goodman, ex-pugilist and pedestrian, and actual tailor', who occasionally came down to teach his art. He dwells nostalgically over the time when 'Burk—the fighting man . . . the "Deaf'un", as he was called', honoured Oxford with his presence and allowed himself to be 'too copiously treated' to the point that he invited his admirers to strike him at 'half a crown a hit'. Burton reports wonderingly that 'we all tried our knuckles upon his countenance, and only hurt our own knuckles'. But the boisterous, rowdy, and callous Burton could go to the other extreme as well; he could, for example, wax 'tender and aesthetic', if not 'sentimental', over Newman's sermons. Concerning Newman he felt that 'there was a peculiar gentleness in his manner' and that 'there was a stamp and seal upon him, a solemn music and sweetness in his tone and manner, which made him singularly attractive'.

No short sketch of Burton, it seems to me, can come closer to an epitome of the man's temper than does the impression offered by a consideration of these extremes of feeling. Almost everywhere in Burton the reader is surprised by this curious mixture of coarseness and tenderness, by a tension between a fascination for what is earthy and a genuinely sympathetic appreciation of what is 'sentimental, tender, and aesthetic'. Tension *is* the better word; for I think it was the inability of these two attitudes to mix well and modify each other that made Burton so unconventional. And at no time was Burton's conduct more unconventional than it was during his short stay at Oxford. From the first time he passed through the entrance of Trinity College when he felt obliged to call out a fellow student who had laughed at his splendid moustache, to his defiant exit on the forbidden tandem after deliberately bringing about his own rustication, Burton was conspicuously out of place. He was disgusted at the student's refusal of his challenge; he felt that he had fallen among a people devoid of all honour. And although the immediate cause of his dismissal was his attendance at a forbidden race, he had sorely tried the patience of officials from the time of his arrival at Trinity. Partly because of his unconventional attitude and partly because the outbreak of the Afghan War had raised to fever pitch the boy's ceaseless pleading for military service, Burton's father at last provided his son with a commission in the Indian Army—a commission which, according to Burton's later estimate, cost his father 500 pounds.

Burton was twenty-one years old on June 18, 1842, when he embarked for India to join the Indian service. From then until his death in 1890 while serving as Consul at Trieste, he explored hitherto unknown regions of four continents, constantly

Richard Francis Burton—Hajï

in the face of great danger and hardships, and produced some fifty volumes of prose and verse. His bibliography presents an amazingly accurate account of his biography for this period.[3] From his first publications in the Journal of a Bombay branch of the Asiatic Society ('A Grammar of the Jataki or Belochki Dialect', 'A Grammar of the Multani Language', and 'Critical Remarks on Dr. Dorn's Chrestomathy of Pushtu, or the Afghan Dialect'—all in 1849) to the printing of his translation and annotation of the *Arabian Nights* between 1885 and 1888, his books tell the story of a wandering spirit with a phenomenal capacity for mastering languages. Four books in 1851 were the result of his experiences in India; the *Personal Narrative of a Pilgrimage to Mecca and El-Medinah* (1855) is perhaps his best effort in the genre of travel literature; between 1855 and 1864 six works narrating his experiences in Africa were published; his views on the Mormons, formed on a trip across the North American Continent, appeared in *The City of Saints* (1861); his consulship in Brazil provided opportunities for excursions into South America and, of course, several books, two of which were *The Highlands of the Brazil*, in 1869, and *Paraguay*, in 1870; in the next two years he published books and articles on Syria and Zanzibar; *Ultima Thule: a Summer in Iceland* came in 1875; a trip back to India produced *Sind Revisited* in 1877; in each of the following two years he issued a book on the gold mines of Midian in Arabia; and finally, in 1883, appeared his last travel-book, *To the Gold Coast for Gold*.

From the great mass of Burton's writings three works stand out: the *Pilgrimage* as his outstanding contribution to travel literature; the *Thousand Nights and a Night* as his most important translation and as a mine of 'anthropological' information; and the *Kasîdah* (1880), a long poem representing his best attempt at creative literature and perhaps the most self-revealing. Besides representing Burton's love of adventure and travel and his phenomenal ability with languages, these three works are those most directly concerned with Arabic culture and most indicative of the author's temperament. And it is with that temperament and with the way in which it was affected by the impact of Arabic culture that this chapter is concerned.

Richard Francis Burton—Haji

2

The mere awareness of the circumstances of time and place surrounding his travel-books is enough to impress one with Burton's fearless wanderlust. In some of the areas Burton was the first white visitor, as in Harrar in East Africa and the lake regions of Central Africa; in others, he appeared soon after the first occidentals, as in Northwest India (what is now Pakistan) and at Mecca and Medina. But whether or not he was the first white visitor, he always seems to have been the most thorough one. He posed as a native in India with such success that he was able to gain information from even the women's quarters of households, and though he was preceded by other Europeans in his pilgrimage to the Moslem holy places, he was the first to pretend to be a Moslem and to be thus enabled to learn the innermost secrets of the Moslem ceremonies. Lodovico Bartema from Rome in 1603, Joseph Pitts from England in 1680, Giovanni Finati from Italy and Burckhardt from Switzerland, both in 1814, were not so successful. But for a clearer understanding of Burton's fascination with travel and adventure we must turn to his own descriptions. Although an adequate appreciation can be gained only from an extensive reading of Burton's books, the following specimens serve to illustrate what I think are four of the most important ingredients in his fascination with travel in the East.

The mystery and melancholy of the East seems to have held the greatest fascination for him:

> Wonderful was the contrast between the steamer and that villa on the Mahmudiyah canal! Startling the sudden change from presto to adagio life! In thirteen days we had passed from the clammy grey fog, that atmosphere of industry which kept us at anchor off the Isle of Wight, through the loveliest air of the Inland Sea, whose sparkling blue and purple haze spread charms even on N. Africa's beldame features, and now we are sitting silent and still, listening to the monotonous melody of the East—the soft night-breeze wandering through starlit skies and tufted trees, with a voice of melancholy meaning.
>
> (*Pilgrimage*, I, 8–9)[4]

Richard Francis Burton—Haji

Perhaps one needs more than a superficial acquaintance with Burton in order to appreciate the sincerity which lies behind this now superficial travelogue technique. Seven years of military service in India can do much to dispel the illusions which the romantic element in human nature is prone to create in its imaginings of the strange and exotic; but Burton's romantic inclinations were more than ordinary and his boyhood temperament of sensitiveness and melancholy never left him. Furthermore, this particular fascination which the East held for him was all the more effective because he had never had a sentimental affection for England. Thus the contrast, even in climate and tempo of living as in the above description, is not induced by the exhilaration of mere change. For Burton, who had already had contact with the East, this meeting was in the nature of a reunion of sympathetic temperaments. Like the typical lover, Burton imputed to the beloved the attractions most valued by the lover.

But the East meant excitement, too:

> To the solitary wayfarer there is an interest in the Wilderness [desert] unknown to Cape seas and Alpine glaciers, and even to the rolling Prairie,—the effect of continued excitement on the mind, stimulating its powers to their pitch. Above, through a sky terrible in its stainless beauty, and the splendours of a pitiless blinding glare, the Samun caresses you like a lion with flaming breath. Around lie drifted sand-heaps, upon which each puff of wind leaves its trace in solid waves, flayed rocks, the very skeletons of mountains, and hard unbroken plains, over which he who rides is spurred by the idea that the bursting of a waterskin, or the pricking of a camel's hoof, would be a certain death or torture,—a haggard land infested with wild beasts, and wilder men,—a region whose very fountains murmur the warning words 'Drink and away!' What can be more exciting? What more sublime? Man's heart bounds in his breast at the thought of measuring his puny force with Nature's might, and of emerging triumphant from the trial. This explains the Arab's proverb, 'Voyaging is victory.' In the Desert, even more than upon the ocean, there is present death: hardship is there, and piracies, and shipwreck, solitary, not in crowds when, as the Persians say,

Richard Francis Burton—Haji

'Death is a Festival';—and this sense of danger, never absent, invests the scene of travel with an interest not its own.

(*Pilgrimage*, I, 148-9)

Again, I think, we must consider the description in conjunction with the character of the writer. He had occasion to verify his contrasts through actual experience. He was always happy in personal combat from fisticuffs to swordplay; he faced American Indians on the American prairie, he was attacked and beaten by Arabs, and severely wounded by Somalis; he experienced the threat of shipwreck in the Red Sea and endured illness and constant danger in Eastern and Central Africa. And yet he never had enough of excitement, for it made him feel more alive.

And he derived keen enjoyment from 'mere animal existence':

Though your mouth glows, and your skin is parched, yet you feel no languor, the effect of humid heat; your lungs are lightened, your sight brightens, your memory recovers its tone, and your spirits become exuberant; your fancy and imagination are powerfully aroused, and the wildness and sublimity of the scenes around you stir up all the energies of your soul—whether for exertion, danger, or strife. Your *morale* improves; you become frank and cordial, hospitable, and single-minded: the hypocritical politeness and the slavery of civilization are left behind you in the city. Your senses are quickened: they require no stimulants but air and exercise,—in the Desert spirituous liquors excite only disgust. There is keen enjoyment of mere animal existence.

(*Pilgrimage*, I, 149-50)

Such descriptions as these strike us as resembling his earlier experiences in that they indicate the presence of extremes in Burton's temperament. He could derive almost equally gratifying experience from both his sympathetic imagination and his physical senses.

The final ingredient we shall illustrate is worthy of note only because of its intensity; for the pride which comes from accomplishment is common to man. When after many hardships Burton finally came to the Moslem shrine of shrines in Mecca, he was in ecstasy:

There at last it lay, the bourn of my long and weary

Pilgrimage, realizing the plans and hopes of many and many a year. The mirage medium of Fancy invested the huge catafalque and its gloomy pass with peculiar charms. There were no giant fragments of hoar antiquity as in Egypt, no remains of graceful and harmonious beauty as in Greece and Italy, no barbarous gorgeousness as in the buildings of India; yet the view was strange, unique—and how few have looked upon the celebrated shrine! I may truly say that, of all the worshippers who clung weeping to the curtain, or who pressed their beating hearts to the stone, none felt for the moment a deeper emotion that did the Haji from the far-north. It was as if the poetical legends of the Arab spoke truth, and that the waving wings of angels, not the sweet breeze of morning, were agitating and swelling the black covering of the shrine. But to confess humbling truth, theirs was a high feeling of religious enthusiasm, mine was the ecstasy of gratified pride.

(*Pilgrimage*, I, 160-1)

A sentimental attraction for the melancholy and mystery of the East, the excitement of adventure, the stimulus to keen enjoyment of animal existence, the sense of pride in accomplishment: these were some of the more important spurs to Burton's urge to travel. And when the days of action were past, memory gave an even more attractive aura to the experiences, so that in the Foreword to the *Nights*, Burton called his translation a 'labour of love, an unfailing source of solace and satisfaction' because it bore him like a 'Jinn' back to his past and 'to the land of my predilection, Arabia, a region so familiar to my mind that even at first sight, it seemed a reminiscence of some by-gone metempsychic life in the distant Past'.[5]

But as Stanley Lane-Poole has pointed out in his Introduction to the *Pilgrimage*, 'it is but just to remember that with Burton the passion of the explorer marched *pari passu* with the restlessness of the wanderer: rove he must, but he would rove by preference in untrodden paths, and thus make his love of adventure minister to the advance of geographical science'. Indeed, most of Burton's travels were made possible by the current interest in geography, archaeology, mineralogy, and allied sciences. His travels in Arabia, for example, which form the subject matter of his *Pilgrimage*, were financed by the Royal Geographical Society, while the Indian Government provided him with a year's leave of absence from his military duties in order that he might pursue his study of Arabic where the language might best be studied. His travels in Somali and his mission to Harrar were made possible through pay, expenses, and equipment (though not protection) provided by the East India Company and motivated by purposes geographical and commercial. Again, his travels in the lake regions of Central Africa were under the auspices of the Royal Geographical Society; and his trip resulted in the discovery (though disappointingly enough, not by Burton himself) of Lake Victoria Nyanza, the headwaters of the Nile. Indeed, *The Gold Mines of Midian* and *Midian Revisited* are so full of geographical, ethnological, archaeological, zoological, botanical, and geological data that they might almost be classified with his more direct contributions to the sciences, the numerous articles in geographical and anthropological journals.

3

So much has been made of Burton's travels and his ability to master Eastern languages and customs that his nationality is not given its proper significance. And yet perhaps the most obvious manifestation of Burton's sensibility, after his fascination with travel and adventure, is his intense patriotism. When he explains that the Moslem considers patriotism as part of his religion (*Nights*, II, 183), one is inclined to apply the explanation to Burton himself. For while Burton was not particularly religious in the usual formal sense of the term, that core of guiding concepts by which he lived, like the formal religion of the Moslem, included a real devotion to his birthplace. The patriotism was of a different sort, however, for the Arabic term ('*Hubb-al-Watan*') connotes a warm, sentimental attraction which is not found in Burton. For him the pride in his nationality revealed itself in a mild arrogance; and as might be expected of Captain Burton of the Indian Service, this proud patriotism was part and parcel of a staunch advocacy of British Imperialism.

Anne Treneer would have us believe that Burton 'merged

his nationality and abrogated Christianity in the East'.[6] We may set aside for the moment the charge that he 'abrogated Christianity' and discuss here the problem of the merging of his nationality. Miss Treneer has based her charge on the circumstances of Burton's experiences as related in his *Pilgrimage*. Not only did he make the pilgrimage to Mecca and Medina and take part in all the religious rites there, but he did so without betraying that he was not a Moslem—a betrayal that would have cost him his life. And what is perhaps more remarkable, he passed rigorous tests on the doctrines of Islam in the presence of recognized Moslem theologians. These circumstances go far towards proving that Burton was an Arabist of the highest rank. Besides Arabic, however, he knew most of the languages of the East and a good many of their manifold dialects; he could put on their garments and their mannerisms and pass among the Moslems as one of them. Furthermore, in writing of his adventures, he could discuss their peculiarities, their superstitions, and their customs and conclude that the Arabs were no more enslaved by their foibles than were their brothers all over the world. These things have led Achmed Abdullah to say that Burton was the only Occidental who had solved the 'riddle of the Arab';[7] and these same things, we may suppose, have led Anne Treneer to say that Burton 'merged his nationality'. Now both views have foundation in fact and may be equally substantiated. It is a case of people with different allegiances giving correspondingly different labels to the same phenomenon: Burton's understanding of the Arabs as if he himself were one of them. This is praiseworthy in the eyes of Abdullah; it is despicable for Miss Treneer.

The controversy raised by his disguise as a pilgrim, and especially by his performance of all the religious rites of the Moslems, Burton treated with disdain: 'I recognize no man's right to interfere between a human being and his conscience,' he declared (*Pilgrimage*, I, xxv). Stanley Lane-Poole takes a cautious notice of Burton's decision to disguise himself as a born Moslem rather than as a converted one: 'He would go as a born believer. He seemed to find a moral superiority in the larger, more fundamental deception, and to the casuist the delicate distinction offers a tempting problem.' But Lane-

Richard Francis Burton—Haji

Poole concludes with the admission that 'he is probably within his rights in maintaining that this is a matter which concerns nobody but himself' and insists, 'there can be no question ... that his impersonation multiplied the difficulties of the task. In the new convert much might be excused on the ground of unfamiliarity with the customs, ritual, and language; but the born Moslem had no such refuge.' There were others, of course, who would not believe that Burton could have passed for a born Arab Moslem, but that he must have been considered a British Moslem convert.[8] And there was even circulated a story, scoffed at by Burton, that he had found it necessary to kill a man who had discovered him in the act of performing a function of nature in an unorthodox position.

Whatever the state of his conscience, and whether or not his disguise was entirely successful, Burton constantly made observations which were meant to attest to his understanding of the Arab and which seem to ring true. He was able, for example, to grasp the importance of the apposite use of proverbs in the East;[9] through examples, he could portray quite adequately the 'nervous, excitable, hysterical' Arab temperament;[10] and he was able to appreciate the affectionate nature of the Arabs.[11] An intimate knowledge of their language and philosophical outlook enabled Burton to defend the Moslems against the European charge that they had no sense of gratitude.[12] He instinctively recognized and sympathized with incidents exemplifying true Arab pathos.[13] Like most travellers in the East, Burton was more attracted to the Bedouin tribes than to the settled Arabs; he found their manners free and simple and untainted by 'affectation, awkwardness and embarrassment', those 'weeds of civilized growth' (*Pilgrimage*, II, 85). Although Burton often made those sweeping generalizations which betray insufficient knowledge, he also was discriminating enough to distinguish between the noble Arabs who possessed the 'quality of mercy' and the ignoble who were 'rancorous and revengeful as camels' and not to be trusted (*Nights*, III, 88). While he found the townspeople unattractive, he was still able to point out that the Meccan character is notably 'open to reason' (*Pilgrimage*, II, 236). These and countless other pronouncements show him as an objective observer of Eastern life.

Richard Francis Burton—Haji

But Burton very often coupled his observations with philosophical explanations, and these philosophical generalizations are telling. Note, for example, how he generalizes on the valour of the desert Arab:

> The valour of the Badawi is fitful and uncertain. Man is by nature an animal of prey, educated by the complicated relations of society, but readily relapsing into his old habits. Ravenous and sanguinary propensities grow apace in the Desert, but for the same reason the recklessness of civilization is unknown there. Savages and semi-barbarians are always cautious, because they have nothing valuable but their lives and limbs. The civilized man, on the contrary, has a hundred wants or hopes or aims, without which existence has for him no charms. Arab ideas of bravery do not prepossess us. Their romances, full of foolhardy feats and impossible exploits, might charm for a time, but would not become the standard works of a really fighting people.
>
> (*Pilgrimage*, II, 87)

In passages such as these Burton reveals himself while trying to be objective or 'scientific'. Here, for example, he shows clearly his general position in the nineteenth-century controversy over the origin of man; the reason which he assigns for the alleged caution shown by barbarians and semi-civilized peoples is a good example of his use of hypothetical or rationalized generalizations; and the final comparison tells us something of Burton's pride in his own nationality, for there is no doubt that he looks upon England as a land of 'really fighting people', though temporarily rusty from lack of use.[14] Again, Burton tells something of his temperament when he observes that the people of Medina are characterized by pride, indolence, and an aversion to manual labour, and then goes on to link the growth of industrialism with the decline of chivalry: he agrees with the Arab aversion to labour for 'there *is* degradation, moral and physical, in handiwork compared with the freedom of the Desert', and 'the loom and the file do not conserve courtesy and chivalry like the sword and the spear'. For when a man has no fear of being killed for his insolence he is prone to be insolent. It is clear, he thinks, that the revolver has made even the ruffian of California polite and that 'those European Nations who were most polished when every gentleman wore a rapier, have become the rudest since civilization disarmed them' (*Pilgrimage*, II, 10).

Burton's sympathetic understanding of the Arab is also seen in his frequent cross references to European chivalric tradition and its sources. He relates the Arab in his readiness to shed tears to the Italians of Boccaccio and to the heroes of Homer (*Nights*, I, 68); he observes that 'from ancient periods of the Arab's history we find him practising knight-errantry, the wildest form of chivalry' (*Pilgrimage*, II, 95); he explains that 'in the days of ignorance, it was the custom for Badawin, when tormented by the tender passion, which seems to have attacked them in the form of "possession," for long years to sigh and wail and wander, doing the most truculent of deeds to melt the obdurate fair' (*Pilgrimage*, II, 96). All of this, combined with what he observed of poetic nature[15] and Platonic affection[16] among the Arabs, tempted him to assign to Arabic influences the origin of 'love'. And he would have succumbed to the temptation 'were it not evident that the spiritualizing of sexuality by sentiment, of propensity by imagination, is universal among the highest orders of mankind'. Those who would attribute the origin of love to the influence of Medieval Christianity seem to forget that 'certain "Fathers of the Church" ... did not believe that women have souls'. The Moslems, he asserts, 'never went so far' (*Pilgrimage*, II, 92).

Finally, Burton betrays his attraction to Eastern life in describing what he calls the untranslatable 'Kayf' of the Arab:

> And this is the Arab's *Kayf*. The savouring of animal existence; the passive enjoyment of mere sense; the pleasant languor, the dreamy tranquility, the airy castle-building, which in Asia stand in lieu of the vigorous, intensive passionate life of Europe. It is the result of a lively, impressible, excitable nature, and exquisite sensibility of nerve; it argues a facility for voluptuousness unknown to northern regions, where happiness is placed in the exertion of mental and physical powers; where *Ernst ist das Leben*; where niggard earth commands ceaseless sweat of face, and damp chill air demands perpetual excitement, exercise, or change, or adventure, or dissipation, for want of something better. In

the East, man wants but rest and shade: upon the banks of a bubbling stream, or under the cool shelter of a perfumed tree, he is perfectly happy, smoking a pipe, or sipping a cup of coffee or drinking a glass of sherbet, but above all things deranging body and mind as little as possible; the trouble of conversations, the displeasures of memory, and the vanity of thought being the most unpleasant interruptions to his *Kayf*. No wonder 'Kayf' is a word untranslatable in our mother-tongue.

(*Pilgrimage*, I, 9)

All this is the romantic side of Burton, leading us to suspect that, indeed, Arabia *was* the land of his predilection. But he was an Englishman of the Empire even in describing the characteristics of the Arabs. At first glance it seems important to remember that the *Pilgrimage* is his earliest travel-book success and that the *Nights* is his last great work as we compare the following attitudes to indicate Burton's feelings of patriotism: in the *Pilgrimage* (II, 118), he has high praise for the 'almost absolute independence of the Arabs', comparing it to that of the North American Indians and deciding that the Arab is the more noble race because of its great achievements; but in the *Nights* (X, 67), he berates the 'stolid instinctive conservatism' of the Arab who is a slave to routine despite his 'turbulent and licentious independence which ever suggests revolt against the ruler'. The same quality, 'independence', is romanticized by the Burton of the *Pilgrimage* and condemned by the Burton of the *Nights*. But the time element is not important, for Burton did not grow from the *Pilgrimage* attitude to that of the *Nights*; rather, both attitudes were always present, always producing a tension. The Arab spirit of independence for the most part, and especially when it agitates against the Turkish rule in the Middle East, is admirable; but it must be submissive to British superiority and rule, else it is a spirit of independence which is less than noble.

Burton's imperialistic patriotism is what both Abdullah and Miss Treneer have lost sight of. A realization of this trait will go far in making him less praiseworthy to Abdullah and less blamable to Miss Treneer, and thus bring them closer to a common meeting ground.

Richard Francis Burton—Haji

In his journals (*Life*, I, 16–17), Burton wrote: 'I always acted upon the saying. *Omne solum forti patria*, or, as I translated it, "For every region is a strong man's home."' However, this noble sentiment seems to have been aimed at rather than attained, and desired for its salving properties rather than for its own sake. For in the same journals Burton more emphatically proclaims that no man can be successful in worldly affairs unless he is a representative of his own nation. He complains that he never had the opportunity to understand or be understood by English society whose conditions are so complex that those who would have public careers must 'be broken to it from their earliest day'. And most important, it seems, 'it is a *real* advantage to belong to some parish. It is a great thing when you have won a battle, or explored Central Africa, to be welcomed home by some little corner of the Great World,' for without such roots a man is a stray, 'a blaze of light without a focus' (*Life*, I, 32). This is as close as Burton comes to a sentimental attachment to his country and even here it is allied to his search for recognition, for gratified pride. However, even this qualified love for his native land was not unmixed with criticism. In general, Burton was inclined to prefer government by strong central rule. Even in the most unlikely places he strongly asserts this preference; for example, in the tale of 'King wird Hahn with his Women and Wazirs' in the ninth volume of his translation of the *Nights*, part of the text reads:

> Thus Allah gave them their reward of abjection in this world and prepared them for torment in the world to come; nor did they cease to abide in that murky and noisome place, whilst every day one or the other of them died, till they all perished, even to the last of them.
>
> (IX, 134)

In a footnote to this passage, Burton observes that although this punishment meted out to his wives by the king seems severe, we must remember that Easterns believe in the divine rule of kings and in the king's being the viceregent of God on earth, 'briefly in the old faith of loyalty which great and successful republics are fast making obsolete in the West and nowhere faster than in England'. Taken by itself, perhaps this comment seems ambiguous; but taken in conjunction with other comments, Burton's tone here becomes unmistakable. In another footnote to the *Nights* (VI, 206), for example, he explains that throughout Oriental history, government has been a despotism tempered by assassination and that 'under no rule is man socially freer and his condition contrasts strangely with grinding social tyranny which characterizes every mode of democracy or constitutionalism, i.e. political equality'. Or in another footnote (*Nights*, IX, 94): 'Another instance, and true to life, of the democracy of despotism in which the expressed and combined will of the people is the only absolute law.' As early as the time of his writing of the *Pilgrimage*, Burton showed this same political preference: he observed that Turkish rule in the Holy Land was near its downfall and he attributed this coming event to Turkish bureaucracy, the 'Tanzimat, the silliest copy of Europe's folly' (I, 258–9).

Burton was even more outspoken in his advocacy of British Imperialism. In the Preface to the first (1856) edition of his *First Footsteps in East Africa* he wrote:

> 'Peace,' observes a modern sage, 'is the dream of the wise, war is the history of man.' To indulge in such dreams is but questionable wisdom. It was not a 'peace-policy' which gave the Portuguese a seaboard extending from Cape Non to Macao. By no peace policy the Osmanlis of a past age pushed their victorious arms from the deserts of Tartary to Aden, to Delhi, to Algiers, and to the gates of Vienna. It was no peace policy which made the Russians seat themselves upon the shores of the Black, the Baltic, and the Caspian seas; gaining in the space of 150 years, and, despite war, retaining, a territory greater than England and France united. No peace policy enabled the French to absorb region after region in Northern Africa, till the Mediterranean appears doomed to sink in a Gallic lake. The English of a former generation were celebrated for gaining ground in both hemispheres; their broad lands were not won by a peace policy, which, however, in this our day, had on two distinct occasions well nigh lost for them the 'gem of the British Empire'—India. The philanthropist and the political economist may fondly hope, by outcry against 'territorial aggrand-

izement', by advocating a compact frontier, by abandoning colonies, and by cultivating 'equilibrium', to retain our rank amongst the great nations of the world. Never! The facts of history prove nothing more conclusively than this: a race either progresses or retrogrades, either increases or diminishes: the children of Time, like their sire, cannot stand still.

And in the same Preface, Burton urges further African exploration by appealing to English feelings of national pride. He explains that because of the first attempt the Somalis now know the Englishmen's plans and that a failure to carry them out will mean a disastrous loss of prestige. The loss of life suffered in the first attempt must not be an obstacle to further exploration; all that is needed is proper chastisement of the culprits to command the respect of the people. He asks only for another opportunity, 'an indulgence which will not be refused by a government raised by energy, enterprise, and perseverance from the ranks of a society of merchants to national wealth and imperial grandeur'. And in his journals (*Life*, I, 113–16), Burton inveighs mercilessly against those who were not in sympathy with British Colonial Imperialism. Richard Cobden comes in for special notice as 'one of the most single-sided of men, whose main strength was that he embodied most of the weakness, and all the prejudice, of the British middle-class public', because he found India's government military and despotic, her acquisition the result of unwise violence and fraud, and her financial value to England tenuous. Cobden is attacked especially because he thought it was impossible for England to govern a hundred million Asiatics. He was obviously a 'professional reformer' and his belief that Asiatics should be governed by Asiatics was the 'regular Free-trade bosh'. This mean-spirited man would have been thunderstruck had he heard the laughter with which his utterances were received by white men in India; he could not know, of course, that 'there was not a subaltern in the 18th Bombay N.I., who did not consider himself perfectly capable of governing a million Hindus'. All that was needed was for the English to cease governing their colonies too little, to take their stand as the masters, to declare '*Sic volo, sic jubeo, sit pro ratione voluntas*'. But 'the Government of the Court of Directors was not a rule of honour, and already the hateful doctrine was being preached, that "prestige is humbug" '.

Prestige, of course, is all-important. At the time of the writing of the *Pilgrimage* (II, 231 and 268), Burton foresees the necessity for English occupation of the heart of the Middle East: 'It requires not the ken of a prophet to foresee the day when political necessity—sternest of 'Ανάγκη!—will compel us to occupy the fountain-head of Al-Islam.' And while England was cruel enough not to make Burton a true prophet, by the time of the translation of the *Nights* she was ruling Egypt at least and Burton again deplored the lack of English prestige. The translation itself he informally dedicated to his country in its 'hour of need'. He deplores the overemphasis on Hindu and Sanskrit literature because it had led the English away from the 'Semitic' studies which have the practical value of rendering Englishmen more capable of coping with the Moslems, 'a race more powerful than any pagans'. England must remember that she is the greatest Mohammedan empire in the world and she must cease to neglect Arabism. Her ignorance of Arabic culture and manners has made her rule in Moslem lands a scandal and has exposed her to the contempt of the Eastern peoples and of the Europeans as well. And although Burton and 'a host of others' may 'find it hard to restore England to those pristine virtues, that tone and temper, which made her what she is', at least they can offer her, through their knowledge of the Arab world, the 'means of dispelling her ignorance concerning the Eastern races with whom she is constantly in contact' (*Nights*, I, xxiii-xxix).

With this patriotic purpose, Burton fills his books with suggestions concerning the proper treatment of the Arab. In the *Gold Mines* he distinguishes between the Bedouin and the town-Arab or 'Fellah'. The former he finds 'is still a gentleman in his native wilds. Easy and quiet, courteous and mild-mannered, he expects you to respect him, and upon that condition he respects you—still without a shade of obsequiousness or servility.' Furthermore, 'the Bedawi never tells a lie, and when told one, never forgets it. His confidence is gone forever, and all the suspiciousness of his nature is aroused.' This character portrayal is very practical, of course, for 'should we find it necessary to raise regiments of these men, nothing would be

Richard Francis Burton—Haji

easier. Pay them regularly, arm them well, work them hard, and treat them with evenhanded justice—there is nothing else to do.' And finally, before leaving the subject he ventures the assumption that 'this was the Roman system of garrisoning the forts and outposts to the east and south of Syria'.[17] What could be more natural to Burton than this easy reference to Imperial Rome? Again in the *Gold Mines*, before the British occupation of Egypt, Burton hopes for Egyptian independence from Turkish rule and even for the restoration of Syria to Egypt.[18] By the time of the *Nights*, however, when Egypt is under the rule of England, Burton complains of England's attempt to constitutionalize the Fellah. Burton does not now advocate Egyptian independence; he complains instead of the laxity of English rule, a laxity resulting from European ignorance of the Fellah. He explains that Napoleon Bonaparte, for political reasons, pretended to pity the Fellah and to hate his oppressors the Beys and Pashas, and that this attitude of Napoleon gradually became public opinion. But the 'Fellah must either tyrannise or be tyrannised over; he is never happier than under a strong despotism and has never been more miserable than under British rule or rather misrule'.[19] All these observations occur, characteristically, as a footnote to the passage: 'If I give it to him it will be no light matter to me, and if I give it not, he will torment me; but torture is easier to me than the giving up of cash.' The pertinence of the note to the passage is not evident, it seems to me, but it is not surprising in Burton. Again in the *Nights* (I, 190), and occasioned by the use of the word 'injustice' in the text, an exegesis includes a repetition of one of the sayings of Mohammed that 'Kingdom endureth not with Zulm or injustice'. Burton's conclusion in this note is that the good Moslem will not chafe at infidel rule 'like that of the English, so long as they rule him righteously and according to his own law'.

At times, Burton's concept of justice borders on the cruel. In *First Footsteps* (I, xxxiii-xxxiv), for example, he relates the method of retaliation which he suggested to the authorities at Aden after he had been attacked by the Somalis at Berberah in 1855. Here, of course, allowance must be made for the anger resulting from personal injury, and thus the suggestion that 'these men should be hung upon the spot where the outrage was committed, and that the bodies should be burned and the ashes cast into the sea, lest by any means the murderers might become martyrs' is not hard to understand. One of Burton's companions was killed in this attack, another narrowly escaped death, and Burton himself had his cheeks transfixed by a javelin. It is characteristic of Burton that he made light of his own injury, and in this particular passage he made no reference to it at all. But in the *Nights* (III, 25), his suggestions along similar lines, characteristically dragged in by way of a footnote, appear harsh indeed. The footnote arises from the use of the word 'crucified' in the text. After a short philological observation Burton notes that crucifixion was abolished in the Roman Empire by the 'superstitious Constantine', but practised in the East 'as a servile punishment as late as the days of Mohammed Ali Pasha the Great'. There follows a detailed account of the method by which crucifixion at this time was carried out, the suffering and the humiliation which the victims endured, and the way in which the body was ignominiously left to the carrion birds. Then he adds that since Moslems are not impressed by mere hanging, 'whenever a fanatical atrocity is to be punished, the malefactor should be hung in a pig-skin, his body burnt and the ashes publicly thrown into a common cesspool'.

Burton does not deem such treatment cruel; he considers it not only necessary, but perfectly natural, for he is convinced that the Arabs 'respect manly measures, not the hysterical philanthropic pseudo-humanitarianism of our modern government which is really the cruellest of all'. By way of contrast he cites the policy of Aeyad bin Abihi who reformed Bassorah, which was a den of thieves, in two days of dealing the death penalty and that of the present English Government which could not stem rampant crime in Egypt and which had allowed 'Christian rule' to 'thoroughly scandalize a Moslem land' (*Nights*, IV, 3). And how, then, are the Egyptians to be managed? 'They are to be managed, as Sir Charles Napier governed Sind—by keeping a watchful eye upon them, a free administration of military law, disarming the population, and forbidding large bodies of men to assemble' (*Pilgrimage*, I, 114). This is the harsh, hard, and practical side of Burton which enables him to explain that 'by Moslem law and usage murder

Richard Francis Burton—Haji

and homicide are offences to be punished by the family, not by society or its delegates. This system reappears in civilization under the denomination of "Lynch Law", a process infinitely distasteful to lawyers (whom it abolishes) and most valuable when administered with due discretion' (*Nights*, V, 103). On the other hand, he could see nothing but ruin resulting from the impractical policy of Napier who ordered to be hanged 'every husband who cut down an adulterous wife' in India; for these husbands were British, and their 'offence', after all, was the only way of a man with an unruly wife (*Nights*, IX, 246).

It is not at all illogical that the anti-republican and imperialist Burton should be fortified by a sense of superiority. He considered it a fair lesson in humility to find himself ranked beneath a Eunuch, a 'high-shouldered, spindle-shanked, beardless bit of neutrality', at a gathering of Moslems (*Pilgrimage*, II, 255); he firmly believed that the Bedouin can be inspired with no higher sentiment than fear (*First Footsteps*, I, xxx), and although he saw noble traits in the desert Arab, he had to 'agree with Professor Palmer that the Bedawi ... is like the noble savage generally, a nuisance to be abated by civilization' (*Gold Mines*, pp. 156-7). Not only does he betray a feeling of superiority in virility, sentiment, and degree of civilization, however; by references to slaves and Negroes he very clearly indicates that dignity is not the right of all men. Regarding the Negro, Burton's revealing statement comes by way of a footnote to an episode in one of the tales of the *Nights* in which is given an old legend about the origin of the Negro. The teller of the tale concludes that 'all people are of one mind in affirming the lack of understanding of the blacks, even as saith the adage, "How shall one find a black with a mind?"' Burton dismisses the legend as 'one of those nursery tales in which the ignorant of Christendom still believe', but he agrees with the narrator's observation concerning the Negro's lack of intelligence and finds it 'factual and satisfactory' however much it is 'unpleasant to our negrophils'.[20] Concerning slaves, he observes more or less correctly, I suppose, that throughout the Moslem East the slave held himself superior to the menial freeman; but the tone with which he reminds the 'several anti-slavery Societies' ('honest men whose zeal mostly exceeds their

Richard Francis Burton—Haji

knowledge, and whose energy their discretion') of this fact seems to betray a satisfaction with the *status quo* of slavery and the implied feeling of superiority which makes it acceptable.[21] Finally, I think the tone of the following footnote again gives a subtle hint of Burton's arrogance:

> In parts of West Africa and especially Gorilla-land there are many stories of women and children being carried off by apes, and all believe that the former bear issue to them. It is certain that the anthropoid ape is lustfully excited by the presence of women and I have related how at Cairo (1856) a huge cynocephalus would have raped a girl had it not been bayonetted. Young ladies who visited the Demidoff Gardens and menagerie at Florence were often scandalized by the vicious exposure of the baboons's parti-coloured persons. The female monkey equally solicits the attention of man and I heard in India from my late friend, Mirza Ali Akbar of Bombay, that to his knowledge connection had taken place. Whether there would be issue and whether issue would be viable are still disputed points: the produce would add another difficulty to the pseudo-science called psychology, as such mule would have only half a soul and issue by a congener would have a quarter-soul. A traveller well known to me once proposed to breed pithecoid men who might be useful as hewers of wood and drawers of water: his idea was to put the highest races of apes to the lowest of humanity. I never heard what became of his 'breeding stables'.[22]

These, then, it seems to me, are the most important ingredients of Burton's patriotism. In spite of his lack of a sentimental attraction for his birthplace, due, perhaps, to the circumstance of constant travel in early life, Burton sincerely regrets that his roots had not been more firmly planted in English society. His patriotism makes him impatient with anything that smacks of republicanism or democracy in government. His England is the Empire, pure and simple, without subtle diplomacy and held together by iron rule. And finally, his patriotism includes a feeling of superiority as an Englishman which spills over into a feeling of personal superiority. That this feeling of superiority as a man manifests itself in an undignified attitude toward some of his fellow-men is certainly not to Burton's credit; but it is not to be neglected in any attempt to understand his temperament in general and his patriotism in particular.

4

It is ironic that Burton's imperialistic tendencies were not sufficiently rewarded by British officialdom. Perhaps it is true, as Downey reports (p. 268), that the Government was afraid of Burton's zeal. But there were evidently other reasons for his lack of favour, not the least of which was Burton's reluctance to treat superiors with deference.[23] He was always outspoken and never subservient. He himself attributed official antipathy to the reports he made on vice in Sind while in India under Napier.[24] These reports subsequently became official documents and were allegedly used against him for the rest of his political life. Burton has explained that the reports were instigated by Napier and carried out under his orders, and there is little doubt that this is true. But one may assume, I think, that Burton had no inclination to carry out the task under protest; anyone who has read a substantial amount of Burton is certain to discover that Burton had a fascination with the general subject. In all its many manifestations, this fascination is cloaked with the scientific term (in an age of new and growing sciences), anthropology or 'anthropological notes'.

Needless to say, this has been the focal point of Burton criticism. Most of this criticism, while it may be of some value in determining the temper of the critics, and hence of an age, has little value as an analysis of Burton's temperament; for such criticism is rarely analytical. A fair impression of the range of this criticism can be gained by presenting the extremes. In his romantic treatment of the life of Burton, Downey gives him the sanctions of education, psychology, and religion: he calls him 'a pioneer in sex education, far in advance of his times', who gave to the Western World the benefit of the studies made by Moslems and Easterns in general on 'the art and mystery of satisfying the physical woman'; and he does not neglect to emphasize that many of the Oriental volumes used by Burton concerning this subject were compiled by 'psychologists and religious dignitaries high in office'.[25] Stanley Lane-Poole, on the other hand, has no sympathy with Burton's 'anthropological notes'. He reports that Burton's *Pilgrimage* was saved from the 'top shelf' only by the circumstance of the author's absence from England; 'for Sir Gardner Wilkinson, to whom the manuscript was entrusted, remarked that the amount of unpleasant garbage which he took upon himself to reject would have rendered the book unfit for publication'. The critic's remarks on the *Nights* are devastating: calling the work a 'remarkable performance', he observes that while it is 'a monument of his Arabic learning and his encyclopaedic knowledge of Eastern life', it is equally effective in revealing 'its writer's astonishing familiarity with the *argot* and "Billingsgate" of the Arabs, no less than with their most secret, and, it must be added, most disgusting habits'; and while it is a witness of the author's profound knowledge of the language and customs of the Arabs, it testifies 'no less clearly to an attitude of attraction towards all that is most repulsive in life and literature'. He finds that the anthropological notes 'evince an intimate acquaintance with Oriental depravity, the confession of which has at best the merit of boldness, whilst the elaborate exposition of so much filth can scarcely be matter of congratulation'.[26] Besides representing the other extreme, Stanley Lane-Poole has touched here, I think, the pulse of Burton's 'anthropological notes': Burton's 'attraction' towards the subject. That the subject is called 'all that is most repulsive in life and literature', however, bears witness to the temperament of Lane-Poole, I should think, and not necessarily to that of Burton.

Burton's defence against such criticism is the richest source of clues to his temperament. At the end of the final volume of his *Supplemental Nights*, in over one hundred pages of reduced type, he has produced what he calls 'The Biography of the Book and Its Reviewers Reviewed'. Approximately half of this section is devoted to quotations from favourable reviews, or to favourable portions of reviews. But far more interesting is the other and first half. Nowhere in these pages is there any sign of reticence, reserve, the silence of contempt, or devastating subtlety; the retaliation is vitriolic, sometimes carping, and often childishly *ad hominem*. One is startled by the quotation from the mild-mannered Darwin which is subscribed on the title page of this essay, for it is only superficially apposite.[27] The 'Preliminary' to this essay is in part an apology for the retaliation: the author has spent a third of a century in the production of his translation, 'half the life of average men and the normal endurance of a generation'; this fact alone should entitle him to some notice of the book's reception by 'critics, reviewers, and criticasters'. Furthermore, 'to ignore the charges and criminations brought forward by certain literary Sir Oracles would be wilfully suffering judgment to go by default'. For however unpopular may be the 'criticism of critique', the author holds it as his 'bounden duty, in presence of the Great Public, to put forth his reply, if he have any satisfactory and interesting rejoinder, and by such ordeal to purge himself and prove his innocence unless he would incur wittingly impeachment for contumacy and contempt of court'. And very characteristically,

> To ignore and not to visit with *représailles* unworthy and calumnious censure, may become that ideal and transcendental man who forgives (for a personal and egoistical reason) those who trespass against him. But the sublime doctrine which commands us to love our enemies and affect those who despitefully entreat us is in perilous proximity to the ridiculous; at any rate it is a vain and futile rule of life which the general never thinks of obeying. It contrasts poorly with the common sense of the pagan—*Fiat Justitia, ruat caelum*; and the heathenish and old-adamical sentiment of the clansman anent Roderick Dhu—
> 'Who rights his wrong where it was given,
> If it were in the court of Heaven,'
> *L. of the Lake*, v. 6.
> —commends itself far more to what divines are pleased to call 'fallen human nature' that is the natural man.

Having thus established his right to speak, Burton proceeds to lash out at six 'unfriends': The *Pall Mall Gazette*, the *Echo*, the *Saturday Review*, what Burton calls the 'Lane-Poole clique', the *Edinburgh Review*, and 'The Critic in America'.

The *Pall Mall Gazette* receives the full treatment *ad hominem*, beginning with the name-calling technique ('Sexual Journal' and 'Gutter Gazette', among others) and ending with a parting shot at the editor, William T. Stead, who had defended a cold-blooded murderer and did not have the 'manliness to apologize' after the murderer confessed his guilt and was hanged. In between, by way of explaining the motives of the *Pall Mall*'s attacks upon him, Burton after long labour gives rebirth to a scandal already three and a half years dead which began with a series of articles in the *Pall Mall* called 'The Maiden Tribute of Modern Babylon'. The most charitable motive which Burton can assign to the editor for printing these sensational articles on vice in London is that Stead was seeking to increase circulation which had fallen off because of his 'exaggerated Russophilism and Anglophobia'. These articles were collected in a twopenny pamphlet entitled 'Report of the *Pall Mall Gazette's* Secret Commission' which Burton soundly berated for corrupting youth at home and damaging English prestige abroad. Soon after the appearance of the pamphlet, Stead was involved in the Eliza Armstrong case. Evidently to prove his sensational charges concerning the corruption of London, Stead had an accomplice go out 'to procure a maiden'. This turned out to be a kidnapping, however, and Stead was given a prison sentence of three months for being the chief plotter in the affair. In relating this episode, Burton finds occasion for some harsh words about 'Methody' which liberally supplied the 'Stead Defence Fund' and about the National Vigilance Association, 'a troop of busybodies captained by licensed blackmailers'. After this long *narratio*, Burton comes to his main argument: while Stead was still in prison Burton was asked for an interview by the sub-editor of the *Gazette*, Mr. Morley, Jr. Not wishing to be associated with the editor, Burton refused to co-operate with the would-be interviewer and consequently was subjected to the attacks of a German Jew who signed himself 'Sigma' in two articles: 'Pantagruelism or Pornography?' (September 14, 1885) and 'The Ethics of Dirt' (September 19, 1885). Burton gives the articles themselves only the attention necessary to quote their titles and dates and to fling the epithet 'German Jew' at their author. The rest of the eight pages devoted to answering the first 'unfriend' consists of a profoundly bitter attack on the character of the *Gazette* and on the base motives of its editors.

Perhaps because at the time of its attacks (October 13 and 14, 1885) it was 'diminutive', and no doubt because by the time of Burton's answer (1888) it had 'made a name for decent and sensible writing, having abandoned the "blatant" department to the *Star*', the *Echo* is treated with comparative mercy. At any rate, it merits only one short paragraph in Burton's essay. The *Echo* had unwisely followed the suit of the *Pall Mall Gazette* by asserting that Burton was 'always eager after the sensational' and that in the *Nights* he was catering 'for the prurient curiosity of the wealthy few'. Burton quotes the final passage of the article in question, adding punctuation in parenthesis and a terminal comment to show his disdain:

'Captain Burton may possibly imitate himself (?) and challenge us (!) to mortal combat for this expression of opinion. If so, the writer of these lines will imitate himself (?) and take no notice of such an epistle.(') The poor scribe suggests the proverbial 'Miss Baxter, who refused a man before he axed her'. And what weapon could I use, composing-stick or dung-fork upon an anonymous correspondent of the hawkers' and newsboys' 'Hecker', the favourite ha'porth of East London? So I left him to the tender mercies of *Gaity* (October 14, '84):—

> The *Echo* is just a bit wild
> Its 'par.' is indeed, a hard hitter:
> In fact, it has not drawn it mild;
> 'Tis a matter of 'Burton and bitter'.

The *Saturday Review*, 'this ancient dodderer, who has seen better days', the 'Saturday Reviler', is the third 'unfriend'. The reviews in this periodical considered certain words and phrases in Burton's translation 'too conceited to be passed over without comment'. Burton lists these as 'the good old English "whenas", the common ballad-term "a plump of spearmen" and a "red cent", the only literal rendering of "Fals ahmar" which serves to show the ancient and noble pedigree of a slang term supposed to be modern and American'. For considering these terms conceited, the *Saturday Review* is described as permanently characterized by 'carping criticism, wrong-headedness and the *culte* of the common-place'. Another reviewer has the audacity to begin by stating that all people are reluctant to receive advice and by applying this dictum to Burton. Burton, after noticing two grammatical errors in the article, points out that the 'sentiment is the reverse of new', quotes *The*

Spectator (No. dxii) where the same sentiment is expressed, and adds, 'but Mr. *Spectator* writes good English and his plagiarist does not'. And before leaving the *Saturday Review*, Burton sums up its inglorious history:

> Like other things waxing obsolete it has served, I hasten to confess, a special purpose in the world of letters. It has lived through a generation of thirty years in the glorification of the mediocrities and in pandering to the impish taint of poor human nature, the ungenerous passions of those who abhor the novel, the original, the surprising, the startling, and who are only too glad to witness and to assist in the Procrustes' process of trimming and lengthening out thoughts and ideas and diction that rise or strive to rise above the normal and vulgar plane. This virtual descendant of the ancestral Satirist, after long serving as a spawning-ground to envy, hatred and malice, now enters upon the decline of an unworthy old age.

Burton uses twenty-eight pages of his essay to answer the *Edinburgh Review* and the 'Lane-Poole clique'. With very painstaking detail he points out the review's glaring errors, misstatements, and ignorance concerning the history of the translation of the *Nights*. He quite convincingly shows also the absurdities of the review's glorification of Lane's translation and its depreciation of Payne's. Nonetheless, Burton again makes use of name-calling (*'Edinburgh criticaster'*) and harsh invective. Stanley Lane-Poole is a 'parlous personage', a 'sapient criticaster, with that normal amenity which has won for him such honour and troops of unfriends: when his name was proposed as secretary to the R.A.S., all prophesied the speediest dissolution of that infirm body'. And after so many pages of energetic defence, Burton concludes with an implicit denial of what he is expressly affirming: that he is not so 'thin-skinned' as to be disturbed by the *Edinburgh's* 'envy, hatred and malice'. But he *is* disturbed and he seeks refuge by allying himself with Macaulay, Darwin, Huxley, and Hooker, all of whom had been attacked by the *Edinburgh*. And most obviously, of course, he is disturbed to the extent that he indulges in very uncomplimentary character portrayals of the editor, Mr. Henry Reeve.

The American Press comes in for the same sort of treatment

and, of course, some of Burton's spleen spills over on to America itself. America is berated for its narrowness and 'indeed the wide diffusion of letters in the States, that favourite theme for boasting and bragging over the unenlightened and analphabetic Old World, has tended only to exaggerate the defective and disagreeable side of a national character lacking geniality and bristling with prickly individuality'. Burton gives a short history of American immigration and concludes: 'to me the wonder is that a poor man ever consents to live out of America or a rich man to live in it.' Furthermore, he finds that America's mixture of all the dregs of the Old World has given her two national characteristics, both 'prejudicial and perilous': 'a splendid self-esteem, a complacency, a confidence which passes all bounds of the golden mean', and 'the glorification of mediocrity'. And finally, concerning America, 'a little learning is a dangerous thing because it knows all and consequently it stands in the way of learning more or much. Hence it is sorely impatient of novelty, of improvement, of originality. It is intolerant of contradiction, irritable, thin-skinned, and impatient of criticism, of a word spoken against it.' All of this criticism may, perhaps, apply to America of the 1880's; the last sentence of it may also apply to Burton.

Burton is calmer and more reasonable when he defends his work in general and not against a particular attack or antagonist. In the 'Foreword' to the *Nights* (I, xiv-xix), he gives a reasonable apology for both his literal translation and for his explanatory notes. He explains that in accordance with his purpose of reproducing the *Nights* 'not virginibus puerisque' but in its original form, he has very carefully chosen the nearest English equivalent for every Arabic word no matter how low or shocking it may be. He insists on the exceptionally high and pure tone of the *Nights* in general, on the devotional fervour which 'often rises to the boiling-point of fanaticism', on the pathos which is sweet, deep, genuine, tender and true, 'utterly unlike much of our modern tinsel', on its poetical justice, and on its sound and healthy morale. But what, then, of the vulgarities and indecencies? Burton tries to show that it is this contrast between the 'quaint element, childish crudities and nursery indecencies and "vain and amatorious" phrase' rubbing shoulders with the passages of complete abandon, 'which forms the chiefest charm of *The Nights*, which gives it the most striking originality and which makes it a perfect expositor of the medieval Moslem mind'. As for his 'anthropological notes', Burton asserts that he cannot imagine *The Nights* being read with profit by men of the West without access to a commentary. And since the specialty of his translation (other translations which are available having other specialties) is anthropology, his notes are necessarily of an anthropological nature. Furthermore, the book provides him with the opportunity to notice 'practices and customs which interest all mankind and which "Society" will not hear mentioned'.

In the 1860's Burton had lent his aid to Dr. James Hunt in founding the Anthropological Society, and had been its first president. His motive was to give travellers the opportunity to publish their 'curious information on social and sexual matters' which is not compatible with the purposes of popular books and which all agree is better 'kept from public view'. But the Society had hardly begun to function, writes Burton, when ' "Respectability," that whited sepulchre full of all uncleanness', frowned upon the members: ' "Propriety" cried us down with her brazen blatant voice, and the weak-kneed brethren fell away.' But 'the organ was much wanted and is wanted still'.

5

There is no doubt that some factual information 'was much wanted'; in no other field could Burton have more profitably exercised his penchant for the 'curious' in human relationships than in the study of Eastern culture. The connotations surrounding the words 'Turk', 'Arab', and 'Mohammedan' have always abounded in sensuality, distasteful to some, appealing and attractive to others. Traditionally in English thought, for example, much had been made of the Moslem concept of heaven with its concomitant physical pleasures.

Burton's notes make a valiant attempt to correct the erroneous view of Occidentals in matters of this nature by explaining tenets of the Moslem faith. He quotes the Koran to prove that Mohammed's Paradise is a spiritual and intellectual condition and that 'only ignorance or pious fraud asserts it to be wholly sensual'. He is convinced also that this paradise is not a greater failure than Dante's and that moreover the Moslems are far more logical than the Christians since they admit into Paradise the 'so-called "lower animals" '. Furthermore, by passing 'over the "Fall" with a light hand', by making man superior to the angels, and by acknowledging, 'even in this world, the perfectability of mankind, including womankind', Mohammed did much to exalt human nature. Christianity suffers by comparison with Islam in this regard; for Islam 'systematically exalts human nature which Christianity takes infinite trouble to degrade and debase', and the fruits of this contrast are painfully evident in the East where the Christians 'are a disgrace to the faith and the idiomatic Persian term for a Nazarene is . . . funker, coward'. Burton explains too that the Moslem considers man superior to woman only in bodily strength, understanding, and the high privilege of Holy War. He blames the Christians for affixing their own early misogyny upon the Moslems in the seventh century. As for the Moslem custom of secluding women, Burton sees in it 'great and notable advantages' though he readily admits that it could not be successfully introduced into European societies. Not the least of its advantages, he finds, is that it abolishes 'such indecencies as the "ballroom *flirtation*"—a word which must be borrowed from us, not translated by foreigners'. Again, polygamy among the Moslems, far from being an example of Moslem sensuality, Burton explains as an extremely just contract between the parties concerned which detracts nothing from the dignity of woman. Indeed, Burton finds that 'nowhere has the sex so much real liberty and power as in the Moslem East'. Furthermore, Burton helps the reader to form a more understanding concept of Moslem polygamy by showing the great need for, and the great value attached to male offspring in the East.[28]

Other practices not fully understood in the Christian West, Burton judges with as much sympathy as he can muster. Circumcision, for example, is praised as a hygenic precaution and as a logical result of professing to follow the lawgiver. In both regards the Moslem is superior to the Christian. When, however, a practice cannot be condoned, Burton tries to minimize Moslem folly by placing beside the Moslem custom an equally unattractive Christian custom. Eunuchry, for example, is coupled with Catholicism's celibate priesthood and both are condemned as abominations. Burton's unqualified praise goes out to Mohammed because he 'did his best to abolish the priest and his craft by making each Moslem paterfamilias a pontifex in his own household and he severely condemned monkery and celibacy'. His comment on chapter iv, verse 81, of the Koran, 'Whatever good betideth thee is from God, and whatever betideth thee of evil is from thyself,' is 'rank manichaeism as pronounced as any in Christendom'; and concerning the attempt in one of the tales of the *Nights* to reconcile man's responsibility with Fate, he finds the writer's 'inability to make two contraries agree as pronounced as that of all others, Moslems and Christians, that preceded him in the same path'. On another occasion he notices that Mohammed has been condemned by some Christian writers for beheading two prisoners, one of whom had spat in his face; the other had recited Persian romances and preferred them to the 'foolish fables of the Koran'. Burton asks, 'What would our forefathers have done to a man who spat in the face of John Knox and openly preferred a French play to the Pentateuch?' And to the charge of idolatry Burton answers, 'But what nation, either in the West or in the East, has been able to cast out from its ceremonies every suspicion of its old idolatry?' and he goes on to list superstitions on the Continent. Although he cannot defend the occasional Mammon-worship at Mecca, he finds the Moslem services are superior in tone and performance to those of Christianity both in the Holy Land and in Rome; for at Mecca one sees no 'silly frauds as heavenly fire drawn from a phosphor-match; nor do two rival churches fight in the flesh with teeth and nails, requiring the contemptuous interference of an infidel power to keep around order'. Nor are there at Mecca curious dames staring through their glasses at the 'Head of the Church', or furtively eating sandwiches during the ceremony, or carrying pampered dogs with them into the church, or scrambling and stampeding like animals in order to listen to 'theatrical music'.

Burton points out that when it was new, Islam 'was at once accepted by whole regions of Christians, and Mauritania, which had rejected Roman paganism and Gothic Christianity' not because it was forced upon them by the sword, 'as is fondly asserted by Christians', but because of 'its fulfilling a need, its supplying a higher belief, unity as opposed to plurality, and its preaching a more manly attitude of mind and a more sensible rule of conduct'. Although Europeans have now forgotten some of the tricks of their former bigotry, they as yet have not profited from a host of books which have sought to clarify a very critical point concerning Islam: 'that the Founder of Al-Islam, like the Founder of Christianity, never pretended to establish a new religion'. Mohammed's aims were merely to correct the manifold abuses into which the Christian religion had fallen. To an unbiased mind, therefore, Mohammed's 'reformation seems to have brought it nearer the primitive and original doctrine than any subsequent attempts, especially the Judaizing tendencies of the so-called "Protestant" churches'. Burton sees the reforming Mohammed finally establishing his religion on two fundamental principles: the unity of the Godhead and the priesthood of the father of the family, principles arising out of a desire to counteract the corruptions of multiple deity and priestcraft which, Burton thinks, characterized the Christian church of the seventh century. And finally, in a detailed defence of Islam against the attack contained in Palgrave's *Narrative of a Year's Journey through Central and Eastern Arabia* (1865), Burton distinguishes Wahhabi-ism, which Palgrave took as representative of Islam, from the true Islamic religion by drawing the parallel between this relationship and the relationship between 'the Calvinism of the sourest Covenanter' and 'genuine and ancient Christianity'.

It seems evident, then, that although 'abrogated' is not the precise word, Burton did do something to Christianity in the East; Miss Treneer's indictment of Burton has some foundation in fact. For in his attempt to correct England's erroneous views of Islam and of Mohammed, Burton continually disparages Christianity.[29] Under Burton's hands, Islam emerges as at least the equal of older faiths and not at all the fantastic and ill-begotten fanaticism of the arch-impostor Mohammed.

Yet, on the other hand, Burton strengthened the traditional concept of the Arabs as rank sensualists. In his 'Anthropological Notes' and in his 'Terminal Essay' of the *Nights*, he gives a very comprehensive survey of sexual perversions in what he calls the 'Sotadic Zone'. The accuracy of the survey and of the explanations is not here open to analysis or question, but there is little doubt, I think, that there is much evidence in Burton's writings to indicate that he goes out of his way to dwell on 'curious' matters which are not the immediate concern of his text. Some instances, in fact, cannot claim the protection of even the very ample mantle of 'Anthropological Notes'. One wonders, for example, if a reference to 'Pope Joan' and the 'papal chair' (*Nights*, II, 80) is the anthropological method of explaining the Arabic phrase 'Kursi alwaladah' or 'birth-stool'. And while the relative significances of a 'man's nose' and 'a maiden's mouth' may be interesting, if somewhat well-known 'anthropological' information, where is the significance of a reference to them when such reference takes the form of a footnote to a description in the text (*Nights*, II, 350) of 'an ancient man, past his ninetieth year; swart of face, white of beard and hoar of eyebrows: lop-eared and proboscis-nosed, with a vacant, silly and conceited expression of countenance' at the sight of whom the Sultan of China laughed? And what a strange association of ideas it is when the story of a Sultan who tries to make peace between a bickering husband and wife by advising them to know each other reminds the translator of the story of an Irishman who through his sexual vigour, 'brought over to the holy Catholic Church' three Protestant wives. Again, when a Sultan rejoices (*Nights*, I, 125) 'with a joy which nothing could exceed' and kisses the eyes of his safely returned daughter, the anthropological note explaining that this is the 'paternal salute in the East where they are particular about the part kissed' is helpful in giving the reader a better understanding of the incident; but of what significance is the additional quotation (from a 'not unusually gross Persian book') regarding a low answer to the question, 'What best deserves bussing?' Burton defends indecencies in the text by appropriating Dr. Johnson's reported 'You must have been looking for them, Madam!' and he justifies his offering of details in his anthropological notes concerning '*Le vice contre nature*' by professing a desire to 'combat a great and growing evil deadly to the birth-rate —the main-stay of national prosperity' (*Nights*, X, 204). Although the analogy in the first argument may limp somewhat (the *raison d'être* of a dictionary not being that of a work of literature), nevertheless, once having granted Burton's right to translate literally, the critic's arguments against indecencies in the text do not taint Burton. If he has a fault, indeed, it is the fault of choosing to translate literally. Similarly, if we grant the patriotic rationalization of the second argument, we can conceivably defend much of Burton's 'Anthropological Notes'. But Burton has supplied us with no argument with which we might defend the poor taste shown in the examples alluded to above; they pertain not to the text nor to England's birth-rate, nor to the medieval Moslem. It is difficult, therefore, not to assume that their significance lies in what they reveal about Burton's temperament.

One of the things about India which impressed Burton was that its 'rank climate, which produces such a marvellous development of vegetation, seems to have a similar effect upon the Anglo-Indian individuality'. He found, for example, that those who were inclined to be irreligious became 'marvellously irreligious', and that those who were previously religious became 'no less marvellously religious'.[30] Perhaps something of the same may be said of Burton. Certainly his boldness shot up marvellously from the time of the *First Footsteps* when he carefully avoided naming venereal diseases in a footnote (I, 126) to the time of the *Nights* when he named them freely; from the time of the *Footsteps* (I, 26) when he considered 'about one-fifth of the Arabian Nights utterly unfit for translation', and when he believed that 'the most sanguine Orientalist would not dare to render literally more than three-quarters of the remainder', to the time of the *Nights* when he not only gave a complete literal translation, but confidently expected his readers to agree with him that 'the proportion of offensive matter bears a very small ratio to the mass of the work', and defended the *Nights* by reminding his readers of the Old Testament's 'allusions to human ordure and the pudenda, to carnal copulation and impudent whoredom, to adultery and fornication, to onanism, sodomy and bestiality' (X, 253-4).

6

This view of the Bible, of course, is a highly specialized one, calculated to confound his critics. And yet, the tone of irreverence is not forced, for Burton had no faith in Judaism or Christianity. Likewise, it should be kept in mind, I think, that

Burton's praise of Islam was similarly motivated. His disguise as a Moslem was not only criticized as deceitful, but also as disgraceful and beneath the dignity of a Western Christian. Thus he exalted Islam at least partly in answer to Western bigotry and ignorance. But of course he was no true Moslem.

In his two autobiographical essays, the one written for Hitchman in 1888 and the one dictated to Mrs. Burton in 1876, Burton mentions his connections with Roman Catholicism while he was at Goa in India as a subaltern. No details are given; he remarks merely that he astonished his comrades by leaving off ' "sitting under" the garrison Chaplain', and transferring himself 'to the Catholic Chapel of the chocolate-coloured Goanese priest, who adhibited spiritual consolation to the bultrels (butlers and head-servants) and other servants of the camp'.[31] The year is 1843 and the motive for his mentioning this activity seems to be the desire to explain his mingling with the natives in order to study them. Nothing more, I think, can be inferred. Mrs. Burton, who would certainly have made much of this passage if anyone could, contents herself with reminding her critics that this occurred before she knew her husband and that he never told her about it until long after they were married. She does, however, report his saying (*Life*, I, 123), 'if a man *had* a religion, it must be the Catholic; it was the religion of a gentleman—a terrible religion for a man of the world to live in, but a good one to die in'. In answer to her critics who asserted that she was falsely representing her husband to be a Catholic, Mrs. Burton reminds them that she 'never called him a devout practical Catholic; I only said he was received into the Church, and that he meant to have its rites at the time of his death'.[32] In the introduction to her *Life* of her husband, Mrs. Burton explains that her critics appear in the form of letters signed 'Anonymous' or 'Agnostic' but that she cannot satisfy them by calling her husband an 'English Agnostic'. She asserts that her husband was a 'Master-Sufi' and explains the term in an attractive, if inadequate, description of 'Sufi-ism'.

Trying to give Burton's religious and philosophic beliefs a label is as unprofitable as it is difficult. Yet the beliefs themselves are easily ascertained, for the *Kasîdah* amounts to a philosophical and religious treatise, and in spite of the F. B. (Frank Baker) pseudonym and the pretence that the poem is a translation, there is no doubt that Burton is very seriously setting forth in it his own views. By means of a Preface, a section of notes on the 'author' and another section of notes on the poem itself, a total output exceeding the length of the poem, Burton shows how seriously he means the work to be taken. And while the poem was written in 1853 and first published in 1880, nowhere in his later writings does Burton contradict its tenets. In outlining his philosophical and religious outlook, therefore, we may draw from both the *Nights* and the *Kasîdah* without making an issue of the dates.

Perhaps the greatest shortcoming of both Christianity and Judaism, according to Burton in the *Nights* (X, 185), is that they utterly ignore 'the progress of humanity, perhaps the only belief in which the wise man can take unmingled satisfaction'. This shortcoming irritates Burton's sense of the dignity of man, a dignity which is inextricably entangled with Burton's sense of personal pride. The combination can be seen more clearly, perhaps, in his criticism (*Nights*, V, 196) of Christians 'who are the only worshippers who kneel as if their lower legs were cut off and who "join hands" like the captive offering his wrists to be bound (dare manus)', and of the Moslem prostration 'which made certain North African tribes reject Al-Islam, saying "These men show their hind parts to heaven." ' Nevertheless, he recognizes the universality of 'Faith ... the *sensus Numinis* which ... is so far divine that it primarily discovered for itself, if it did not create, a divinity'. Hence he disagrees with Novalis' Christ who cries 'Children, you have no father', and he joins Renan in crying *'Un monde sans Dieu est horrible!'*[33] But because of what seem to him the endless contradictions springing from a belief in a Personal God, Burton must take 'refuge in the sentiment of an unknown and unknowable' (*Kasîdah*, p. 68).

The greatest of these 'contradictions' is the existence of Divine foreknowledge side by side with human free will; according to Burton, this problem disappears when we substitute Law for a personal Deity (p. 84). Such a Law enables him to hold a 'modified fatalism', a fatalism that seems to be analogous in some ways to the 'proud resignation to the decrees of Fate and Fortune' which he found so ennobling in Al-Islam (*Nights*, X, 64). He believes with Lamarck that the will is never really free; that man is 'a co-ordinate term of Nature's great progression, a result of the interaction of organism and environment, working through cosmic sections of time'; that the word 'mind' is a convenient term describing a 'special operation of matter'; that man's faculties are the outward signs of the action of the central nervous system; and that 'every idea, even of the Deity', is 'a certain pulsation of a certain little mass of animal pap—the brain'. Therefore, he has no objection to being related to the ape, and more important, since he came into the world not of his own free will and since he is here subject to laws and circumstances which he had no part in establishing, he himself cannot be held responsible for his actions. 'I feel, I know that Fate *is*,' he explains, 'but I cannot know what is or what is not fated to befall me.' This inability to know what is in store is a clear indication to Burton that his highest and only duty is the 'pursuit of perfection'. He cannot make himself believe in a 'self-less man', which to him denotes 'an inverted moral sense'. He is morally bound to weigh carefully the possible consequences of his every word and deed; but, when 'the Future has become the Past', it would be 'the merest vanity for a man to grieve or to repent over that which was decreed by universal Law'. And as with repentance, so with conscience: the 'incentive to beneficence' involved in these concepts is to be applied to the future, not to the past. (*Kasîdah*, pp. 80–3.)

From the *Kasîdah* we learn that as for a future life, sentiments and affections seem to demand it; but this sentiment is by no means universal, for the Buddhists, Turanians, and Confucians deny, ignore or protest against the idea, and its votaries cannot deny that it is always conceived as but a copy of this world more or less idealized. The Prophet, for example, showed great wisdom in making his Paradise for the poor consist of splendid eating and drinking, for the half-famished Bedouin think of nothing beyond the stomach and their dreams can know no higher bliss than 'mere repletion'.[34] While not denying the possibility of immortality, Burton regrets in the *Kasîdah* (pp. 71–72) that so much importance is given to the idea, because it is a sort of artificial 'psychical stimulant' which hinders the orderly progression of man's life here and now. And in the absence of proof, the wise man should suspend his judgment, should 'cultivate that receptive mood which, marching under the shadow of mighty events, leads to the highest of goals—the development of humanity'. The spiritualists' phrase, 'passed away to a higher life', embodies a theory not at all proved, and yet Spiritualism thrives, 'despite the Medium', because its idea of a future state is 'the only possible and intelligible' hypothesis offered for a future existence (*Nights*, IX, 54 and 86). And so one of his volumes (VII) of the *Nights* is dedicated to 'Frederick Hankey, Formerly of No. 2, Rue Laffite, Paris', by way of a cautiously worded message: 'If there be such a thing as "continuation", you will see these lines in the far Spirit-land and you will find that your old friend has not forgotten you and Annie.'

'Spiritualist,' however, like most other terms, does not fit Burton with any great accuracy. Lady Burton (II, 137–57) quotes her husband's lecture delivered before the British National Association of Spiritualists in December 1878; it is marvellously non-committal on his own belief in Spiritualism. He does recount his experiences with spiritualistic phenomena in the East, however, and calls Spiritualism a 'Zoo-electric force' which no doubt will be an important field of investigation for future scientists. In the *Nights* (III, 346) he indicates that he has seen and heard of so many 'miracles' in the East that the power cannot be disregarded; and he observes (X, 26) that a frequently occurring phenomenon is the 'abnormal introvision and divination of things hidden which are the property and prerogative of perfect love'. Although Burton alludes to matter as eternal, and although he looks upon Berkeley as a casuist, he cannot be classified as a rank materialist. He states emphatically in the *Kasîdah* (pp. 69 and 90) that the soul is not material; it is not a thing, but a 'state of things' denoting 'the sense of personality, of individual identity'. Furthermore, he attaches great importance to 'the sentiments, the affections which are, perhaps the most potent realities of life'.

Burton admits (*Nights*, I, 249) that there is much that cannot now be known; Truth itself is not fully known and 'the great question still remains, What is Truth?' But truth must be sought, 'truth only, truth as far as man, in the present phase of his development, is able to comprehend it'. Burton disdains to associate truth with utility as Bacon has done; he sees thought injured by the '*a posteriori* superstition, the worship of "facts", and the deification of synthesis'; and he regrets that Locke recklessly broke with the past in refusing the philosophy of innate ideas, for by doing so Locke aided that movement called Progress which 'has often been retrograde' and abetted 'the development of egotism resulting from the pampered sentiment of personality' (*Kasîdah*, p. 71). Truth must be worshipped for its own sake, not for any reward and not for the service it might do for any system or theory.

And as with Truth, so must it be with Goodness; 'the bribe and threat doctrine', the attitude of mind which holds that 'the abstract idea of goodness is not an effectual motive for well-doing', is ignoble (*Nights*, X, 183-4). Further, actions themselves are good or bad only relatively; 'for morality is, like conscience, both geographical and chronological' (III, 24). Burton in the *Kasîdah* (pp. 75-7) protests strongly against the doctrine of 'original sin', Newman's 'original calamity', held by Catholics and even by the 'most liberal Christian Church' whose Schedule of Doctrines 'insists upon human depravity'. This theory is unscientific and so is the belief that evil came into the world with Adam and his seed. For before Adam the world was full of monsters and 'the Law of murder' was 'the Law of Development'. All this natural cruelty and destructiveness of things can be explained only by a Law without a law-giver, and any attempt to reconcile the idea of an Omniscient Law-giver with the existence of evil is doomed to failure. But Burton believes with Augustine that 'Absolute Evil is impossible because it is always rising up to good', and, 'as F. W. Newman says, "so likewise is Evil the revelation of Good" '. All existence is equal, so long as it has the 'Hindu Agesa, Life-fluid or vital force'; Pope shows great wisdom with his 'harmony not understood' and his 'All partial evil universal good'.

And yet, who can deny that there is misery in the world? Burton can only wail over its prevalence and 'assume its foundation to be error, and purpose to abate it by uprooting Ignorance which bears and feeds it'. For life, whatever it may lead to, 'is built upon a basis of sorrow'. Does not 'literature, the voice of humanity, and the verdict of mankind proclaim that all existence is a state of sadness'? With Cardinal Newman, 'one of the glories of our age', Burton finds ' "the Light of the world nothing else than the Prophet's scroll, full of lamentations and mourning and woe" '. But Burton also borrows from Buddhism in attempting to solve this problem of happiness and misery: they are equally divided in an individual and in the world as a whole; for the 'highest organisms are most susceptible to the highest pleasures as well as the deepest woes', and so 'the beggar is, on the whole, happy as the prince'. And if one asks what is the advantage of trying to elevate one's intellectual and spiritual capabilities, Burton can only answer, 'Such is the Law' and we must obey. He explains his view of life as 'that of the Soofi, with the usual dash of Buddhist pessimism. The profound sorrow of existence, so often sung by the dreamy Eastern poet ... a healthy wail over the shortness, and the miseries of life.' The only consolation is to be found in 'self-cultivation, and in the pleasure of the affections'. The affections, he indicates, include 'the sympathies and the "divine gift of Pity" '.

This is the message which Burton as translator claims his author means to deliver; it is 'an Eastern Version of Humanitarianism blended with the sceptical or, as we say now, the scientific habit of mind'.

> Thus he seeks to discover a system which will prove them all right, and all wrong; which will reconcile their differences; will unite past creeds; will account for the present, and will anticipate the future with a continuous and uninterrupted development; this, too by a process, not negative and distinctive, but, on the contrary, intensely positive and constructive.

With an attempt at undercutting irony not altogether successful, Burton comments on this ambition: 'I am not called upon to sit in the seat of judgment; but I may say that it would be singular if the attempt succeeded. ... Meanwhile it satisfies himself,—the main point.'

7

It is unfortunate that in dissecting the traveller-explorer, the imperialist, the anthropologist, and the philosopher we have necessarily murdered Burton. In spite of our frequent use of the author's own words, the warmth, the humanity of the man has escaped our analysis; for the personality of Burton exists not only in the major interests we have examined, but no less in the innumerable minor interests which we have had to neglect. Faced with much the same problem, a more artistic biographer of Burton has noted that 'Every individual face has as many different expressions as the soul behind it has moods'; he concludes that it is the business of the artist to portray none of those many faces, but rather the one which all those many faces have created in the artist's soul.[35] Making no pretensions at art, and risking the danger of oversimplification, we can follow this advice at least to the extent of attempting a synthesis of the various Burtons we have discussed, hoping to arrive at some final statement of the impact of Arabic on the sensibility of the man.

It is the interplay of sensitivity and virility or robustness, I think, which must be the basis for our concept of Burton's temperament.[36] We have seen this combination in the proud and shy boy described by nearly all his biographers and by Burton himself: he was melancholy and sensitive, on the one hand, and prone to every kind of boyish deviltry, on the other. We have also indicated that while he was at Oxford he was impressed not only with the tenderness and sweetness of Newman's sermons, but also with the opportunities afforded for boxing and drinking and for playing every sort of prank. In his contact with the East, we may again divide his attraction into what appealed to his emotions and what appealed to his senses. His ability to master languages and to capture the very spirit of the imagery and idiom testifies to his sensitivity of feelings and to his sympathetic imagination. He was able to become a native to all outward appearances and even to his turn of thought; he understood the Arab to the extent that he could pass as one himself. On the other hand, Burton could become so preoccupied with details that he often was bound by his senses. He so enjoyed robust living, became so deeply impressed with physical facts, that he was often unable to rise above the experience of the facts to their greater significance.[37] Thus, becoming entangled in seeing and feeling, in experiencing life on the mere physical level, Burton often fills his books with 'facts': details ferreted out by his penchant for the curious in human relationships;[38] by his fascination with the dangers of travel, and by his admiration of the opportunities for mere animal existence in the East where one is uncircumscribed by Victorian conventions of society and morality.

This desire for the robust life, Burton tried to put to practical use. We have noted how he relates his knowledge of 'anthropology' to his wish to serve England; by bringing to light sexual perversions, he thinks that he is taking the first step in the fight against the declining birth-rate, that foe to national prosperity. We have seen, too, that he makes his love for travel and adventure serve the cause of geography and allied sciences. It may also be said, I think, that what he found most attractive in the East, its freedom from the conventions of European civilization, he uses as an argument for British Imperialism; for the practical Burton pictured this uncivilized portion of the world as crying for the strong rule of England. Some of his philosophical principles, too, are obviously practical. For example, he conceived the relationship between free will and fate in such a way that he was able to derive from their co-existence the incentive to excel, but in a way too which dispensed with the need for remorse and regret: free will, he emphasized before the deed; fate, once the deed was accomplished.

And yet there was always the tension between the practical, matter-of-fact Burton and the Burton who was attracted by the emotions. In his philosophy he recognized that the affections were, perhaps, the most potent realities, and his view of the world had the thoroughly Eastern basis of a profound sadness for the misery and sorrow of man. And it is this facet of his temperament which gives him his only claim to recognition as an artist. The tension between the two Burtons is perhaps evident in all his writings, but it is only in portions of the *Pilgrimage*, *First Footsteps*, *Kasîdah*, and *Nights*, where the imaginative Burton temporarily overshadows his matter-of-factness, that we have anything worthy of the name of literature. These, of course, are the works most directly concerned with Arabic culture, and we may assume, I think, that it was the subject matter which played the major part in bringing the literary Burton before the reader. Without these works, Burton could claim notice from literature only as a translator of the Portuguese *Lusiads of Camoens*. His thoer works, such as the *Lake Regions of Central Africa* (1860), *City of the Saints* (1861), *Unexplored*

Richard Francis Burton—Haji

Syria (1871), *Gold Mines of Midian* (1878), *Midian Revisited* (1879), and *To The Gold Coast For Gold* (1883) are primarily interesting for the information which they contain about geography, archaeology, mineralogy, and anthropology. These books do not sustain a narrative interest and contain no passages which can compare with the descriptive passages of the *Pilgrimage* and of the *First Footsteps*. But even in these earlier books the writing is unequal in quality and has led critics to deplore his lack of literary talent.[39] Burton himself may have realized that he did not have the artist's touch,[40] for the change in technique between these earlier books and the later ones is too obvious to be unintentional. The *Pilgrimage* and *First Footsteps* contain notes and appendices as do the later books, but the quality of these addenda in the later travel books is more scientific. Finally, the *Nights*, while it contains passages notable for the translator's imaginative grasp of the original, is more famous for the wealth of 'facts' in its 'Anthropological Notes' and 'Terminal Essay' than it is for its display of Burton's sympathetic imagination.

The impact of the East, then, was strong enough to bring into temporary prominence Burton's native imaginative sympathy and emotional sensibility. This is evidenced not only in many passages of the *Pilgrimage* and *First Footsteps* and in the more descriptive couplets of the *Kasîdah* and in rare passages of the *Nights*, but also in some of Burton's views of the world such as in his fatalism, his conviction that life is built on sadness,[41] and his belief that the enjoyment of the affections is the only solace of man. However, it is also evident that the East provided Burton with material to indulge his urge to live robustly, his love for adventure, his penchant for the curious and 'anthropological', and his staunch support of British Imperialism. It may be said, I think, that Burton found everything he needed in the East, or rather, that he was able to turn everything he found in the East to his own use. He was temperamentally susceptible to the romantic charms which the West is prone to ascribe to the East and he fell in love with them; but he was practical and matter-of-fact enough to appreciate the dowry as well.

III

Wilfrid Scawen Blunt—Sheikh

I

ONE can hardly imagine a more grotesque scene than that which depicts Burton in his cups insisting that he try his mesmeric powers on Wilfrid Scawen Blunt, polite diplomatic attaché at the English Embassy in Buenos Aires.[1] 'If I had submitted to his gaze for any length of time—and he held me by my thumbs—I have no doubt he would have succeeded in dominating me,' wrote Blunt thirty-eight years afterwards, 'but my will also is strong, and when I had met his eyes of a wild beast for a couple of minutes I broke away and would have no more.' Burton was forty-eight, Blunt twenty years younger, when the meeting took place in Argentina in 1868. Inasmuch as Blunt kept no journal during the 'sixties, his recollection as set down in 1906 (occasioned by the publication of Wright's *Life* of Burton) may have been influenced and perhaps distorted somewhat by the intervening careers of both men. In 1868 Blunt had as yet no interest in world politics, and Burton's imperialism, though always an integral part of his political views, was not highly publicized until the early 'eighties when the 'Egypt Question' had reached its climax. Then of course, Blunt took an active part in support of Egyptian independence and till the end of his life he spoke loudly and often against British Imperialism. It seems very probable, therefore, that Blunt was more antagonistic towards Burton in 1906 than he was in 1868 when the meeting took place.[2]

Though no reference is made to imperialism, one senses that it is Blunt's repugnance to it which underlies his criticism.

Specifically, he depreciates Burton's feats of travel in two ways: first, by suggesting that the pilgrimage to the Moslem holy cities had not been so difficult of accomplishment as Burton made it out to be in his narrative; and second, by pointedly adding to his account of Burton's announced intention to explore the western Pampas and to ascend the highest summits of the Andes that the highly publicized intention and plans came to nothing more than a source of amusement for his friends. As an introduction to his adverse criticism, he admits that Burton was then 'at the lowest point' of his career 'and in point of respectability at his very worst'; but no other sign of attenuation is evident throughout a detailed account of Burton's addiction to drink ('he seldom went to bed sober') and his resemblance to a 'released convict' in his 'habitual' costume of 'a rusty black coat with a crumpled black silk stock, his throat destitute of collar', all of which was rendered the more 'hideous' by 'his muscular frame and immense chest'. He remembers Burton's face as 'the most sinister' he had ever seen, 'dark, cruel, treacherous, with eyes like a wild beast's'. Still, he adds, Burton's talk was calculated to make him appear more cruel and vicious than he really was: 'even the ferocity of his countenance gave place at times to more agreeable expression'. But 'he showed little true sympathy with the Arabs he had come to know so well. He would at any time, I am sure, have willingly betrayed them to further English, or his own professional interests.' And while he professed materialistic beliefs, there was in him 'a groundwork of belief in the supernatural which refused to face thought's ultimate conclusions'. Burton's literary ability Blunt flatly estimates as second rate.

Many of his criticisms of Burton are objective; and yet it is impossible not to see in the character sketch prejudices which offer clues to Blunt's own temperament. Animosity towards all that is imperialistic, coarse, vulgar, and unsympathetic; an antipathy towards strenuous physical exertion; and a note of selfishness in the pride which thrives on the depreciation of others: these are some of the traits of Blunt's character. But his criticism of Burton also reveals two sympathies which are much more important to an understanding of his thought and work: that for the Arabs and that for the affections connected with love. For Burton is attractive to him primarily because of his travels in the East and especially because of his Arabian adventures; and though Burton's wife 'was indeed a very foolish woman', her biography of her husband 'which has the ring of a true wife's devotion, redeems her' in Blunt's eyes, 'and it is a fine trait' in Burton's character 'that he should have borne with her absurdities for the sake of her love so long'.

Indeed, these two sympathies form the emotional content of most of Blunt's work. When in 1914 Lady Gregory suggested to him that he publish so much of his work as he wished to be made public, he agreed only on the condition that his longer political and philosophical poems be included; he asserted that his poetry had at least the virtue of sincerity, that he had never written merely for the sake of poetry or mere expression, and that he had felt 'as deeply and strongly about certain aspects of what are called world politics' as he had about love: 'My poetry has been my justification in both fields of my active life, not the pursuit of an art for art's sake,' he said.[3] His love poetry is animated by a zest for life and for living; his political verse and prose is motivated by his admiration for the Arab race, by a championing of the cause of freedom all over the world and especially in the East, and by the natural corollary of anti-imperialism.

His versification of the pagan odes of Arabia are in the tone of his love poetry. He caught something of the hedonism and realism of the Arabic and some of its pathos and naïveté. And while there is no satisfactory translation of the *Mu'allakat*, the famous 'suspended odes', Blunt's attempt to recapture the pagan spirit of the original is noteworthy. The most important theme of *The Golden Odes of Arabia* is love, but there are strains also of pathos, excitement of battle, the desire for glory, the pleasures of the senses, and the warmth of Bedouin hospitality. Blunt makes frequent use of transliterations from the Arabic and the usual imitations of imagery and phraseology in order to create the Eastern atmosphere. The very difficult rhymes and metres of Arabic poetry cannot be reproduced in English, for Arabic is exceedingly rich in synonyms and Arabic metres are quantitative rather than accentual; but Blunt uses alexandrine couplets and a frequency of assonance and alliteration in an attempt to imitate the verse movement of the original. His major Eastern verse is his verse rendering of Lady Blunt's translation of *The Stealing of the Mare*. This is a typical Eastern romance, full of love, adventure, and heroic sentiments. The tale is told episodically in prose, and between the prose narrations are unrhymed hexameters which repeat the action and sentiment of the prose. Blunt makes good use of Eastern imagery, but the verse is not outstanding and sometimes flat and prosaic. Here too he was attempting the difficult task of imitating the Arabic metres. The political verse is predominantly anti-imperialistic. *The Wind and the Whirlwind* is the most important of these verses. Written in pentameter quatrains, rhyming *abab*, the verses extol Arabi Pasha as a patriotic reformer who is urging the Egyptians to rise up and free themselves from British domination. Some liberties are taken with the rules of rhyme and in many places rhyme is replaced by assonance. *Satan Absolved* is in the form of a dramatic dialogue and is an even more indignant protest against imperialism. Although these poems, both Eastern and political, do not compare favourably in artistic merit with Blunt's love poetry, they are no less clear in their indication of his sympathies, and they must therefore be considered in any attempt to understand the man.

2

In the pages that follow, the attempt to trace certain patterns in Blunt's temperament in order to determine the effect of Arabic culture on his sensibility will lead us sometimes to cross and then double back over the lines of chronology. Perhaps it will be profitable at the outset, therefore, to resort to the familiar artificial device of dividing the author's life into 'periods'.[4]

He 'began life rather early', he said, being appointed to the diplomatic service at the end of 1858.[5] Born in 1840 into a prominent family of the landed gentry in Sussex, he was the youngest of three children who lost their father in 1842. The restless family then moved about in England from relative to relative and travelled through France in 1846. In the next year the two boys were sent to a private school in Twyford near Winchester where they were very unhappy. In 1851 Mrs. Blunt informed her young children that she had become a Catholic convert and the children were baptized in the following year. At the very beginning of 1853 the boys were sent to the Jesuits at Stonyhurst. In June of that year, shortly after the boys had been removed to Oscott, Mrs. Blunt died. Mrs. Madeline Wyndham, paternal aunt, became guardian of the children; and although not a Catholic herself, she allowed the boys to remain at Oscott until 1857. Wilfrid at this time was launched by his aunt into London society. During the winter he lodged with a couple, the Walfords, in London while he read for the Civil Service examination. He was sent to France for a few weeks to polish his French in the fall of 1858, came back to England and passed the examination for the diplomatic service, and was appointed unpaid attaché on the last day of that year.

He was with the diplomatic service from 1859 to 1869. For a year and a half he was at Athens. When he suffered an attack of fever in August, he received a transfer to Frankfort; but in transit he stopped at Constantinople and was retained in service there for a few weeks. For the almost two years he spent at Frankfort, Miss Finch writes, he was surrounded by 'frankly professed doubters and unbelievers', and was especially troubled by the wife of the Ambassador, Lady Malet, who was constantly speculating on religious problems and discussing *The Origin Of Species* and *Essays and Reviews*.[6] For a short time during the winter of 1862-3 he was stationed at Madrid (he even took an active part in bull-fighting) and for nearly three years between 1863 and 1865 he was at Paris, where he fell passionately in love with a famous courtesan, Catherine Walters—an experience which marked him for life. Towards the end of 1865 he spent a few months in Lisbon where he came under the influence of Lord Lytton ('Owen Meredith'), and he was at Frankfort for a second term in 1866-7. In 1868 his sister accompanied him to his post in Buenos Aires. Early in 1869 he was transferred to Switzerland, and towards the end of the year married Lady Anne Noel, granddaughter of Lord Byron. 'Without regret', he resigned from the diplomatic service two months after his marriage.[7]

Between 1870 and 1875 he suffered the loss of a four-day old son, a wound not completely healed by the later birth of a daughter; mourned the deaths of his beloved sister and brother, which occurred only several months apart; and inherited the Crabbet estates in Sussex. He and his wife made a trip to the

Levant and into Turkish Asia Minor. He fell ill with pneumonia at Constantinople; and when nursed back to health and then pronounced infected with 'galloping consumption', he was given but a few months to live. There was also a year of travel in France and Italy and the publication of *Songs and Sonnets by Proteus* in 1875, verses which he had been writing since the beginning of his diplomatic service.

The following thirteen or fourteen years, Blunt spent in intense political activity. Journeys into Egypt, Arabia, and India between 1875 and 1879 made him conscious of Eastern politics and the burdens placed upon natives by alien despotic rule. His interest in Eastern matters made him socially important in England beginning in 1880, and his *Love Sonnets of Proteus* which he left for Lytton to see through the press in 1880 (published in 1881) increased his fame. In 1881 he became more intimately acquainted at Jidda with Islamic thought, bought a garden of forty acres near Cairo which contained the shrine of a local saint, Sheykh Obeyd, and returned to England to agitate opinion in favour of Egyptian Nationalism. That summer he wrote *The Future of Islam* to set forth what he considered a true picture of Islam and the promise of Islamic reform, and in the next year he produced *The Wind and The Whirlwind*, a long poem in condemnation of the evils and injustices of imperialism. In 1883 he stopped for a few days at Cairo and found himself the rallying point for some of the Egyptian Nationalists who were still in Egypt. He managed to stir up the enmity of Cromer by visiting political prisoners without permission, and Salisbury issued an order excluding him from Egypt for the next three years. He visited the Nationalist exiles in Ceylon, was petitioned for aid by the Moslems in India itself and returned to England in 1884. He now became involved in the Egypt–Sudan question and wrote and spoke incessantly. In 1885 he published *Ideas About India* in which he outlined the inequities and injustices of British rule in India, and suggested the possibility of Indian self-government. He then tried to get a seat in Parliament, but was unsuccessful in the Camberwell elections of 1885 and at Kidderminster in 1886. Dejected, he made a trip to Rome and Italy which is recorded in *A New Pilgrimage*, finally published in 1889. In 1887 he returned to Egypt, came back to England refreshed, and plunged again into home politics. The political issue was Home Rule, about which he had definite views not wholly those of British Imperialism. He accepted the candidacy of Deptford, was arrested and charged with holding a political meeting at Woodford in County Galway, a proclaimed district, and served two months' imprisonment in Kilmainham and Galway jails during which time he lost the Deptford elections. He left prison weary of politics. These experiences produced *In Vinculis* (1899), a collection of poems the major portion of which were written while he was in prison; and *The Land War In Ireland*, not published until 1912.

After 1889 Blunt was very active in society during the London seasons and very happy playing the role of Arab sheikh during the winters at Sheykh Obeyd.[8] In 1892 he versified Lady Anne's translation of the tenth-century Arabian epic, *The Stealing of the Mare*, and wrote the sonnet sequence *Esther*, which he had begun as a blank verse narrative during his Paris days. This volume included 'Natalia's Resurrection' with Blunt's favourite theme of seizing love while it is available, and 'Love Lyrics'. In 1893 he finished *Griselda*, subtitled 'A Society Novel in Rhymed Verse', in inferior narrative couplets, again built around the theme that there is one moment and only one in which love can be realized. His drama, *The Bride of the Nile*, adapting an Arabic account of an incident during the Roman occupation of Egypt to poke fun at Cromer and the British occupation, was written and produced at Crabbet in 1893, and acted at Newbuildings in 1907. Another drama, *The Little Left Hand*, was written in 1897 but never played. *Fand of the Fair Cheek*, written for the actors of the Abbey Theatre, in hexameter couplets as were his previous dramas, was completed in 1902 and privately printed in 1904. This last play drew favourable comment from Yeats. The only previously unpublished verse in the Henley and Wyndham edition of his poetry in 1898 was part of 'Quatrains of Youth'. In 1899 he published *Satan Absolved* using a combination of the *Faust* technique in the 'Prologue in Heaven' and the machinery of the *Book of Job* to condemn English Imperialism. This incorporated some of the ideas suggested by Herbert Spencer in letters to Blunt after the publication of *The Wind and The Whirlwind* in 1882. A poetic version of Lady Anne's translation of the pre-Islamic odes, *The Mu'allakat or Seven Golden Odes of Arabia*, appeared in 1903. The 'Secret History

Series' was published between 1907 and 1920: *Secret History of the English Occupation of Egypt* (1907), *India Under Ripon* (1909), *Gordon at Khartoum* (1909), *The Land War in Ireland* (1912), and *My Diaries* (1919 and 1920). Until 1912 he was engaged in writing numerous articles and pamphlets on these same questions, the most notable of the pamphlets being *Atrocities of Justice Under British Rule in Egypt* (1906). *The Poetical Works, A Complete Edition*, in two volumes, was published in 1914.

Blunt's last residence in Egypt was in 1905. Increasingly failing health sharply curtailed his activities in later life. Beginning in 1896 he began to be alienated from his wife and daughter and there was a definite break with Lady Anne in 1906. A reconciliation was effected in 1915, but the couple was never actually reunited, Lady Anne dying at Sheykh Obeyd in December 1917. In 1922 his very active and very colourful life came to an end and he was buried at Newbuildings in Sussex.

3

The Protean character of Blunt seems to defy analysis. His concern with religion and philosophy was directed towards Catholicism, Modernism, Rationalism, Islam, and Islamic reformation. His experience with love ranged from adulation to sexual love, and to a conception of love as angelic. He was proud, arrogant, and misanthropic; he was compassionate and congenial. All through his life he had a tender regard for animals and a strong love for horses, and he sometimes felt that Nature had only one defect, man. But I think it is possible to trace some pattern in his varied attitudes, and to denote the integration in that pattern of his attraction towards Arabic culture.

The background for Blunt's temperament is a tremendous capacity for sympathy. Father Gerard, when both men were sixty-two, reminded him of their childhood friendship at Stonyhurst and of their habit of keeping caterpillars in paper boxes; Blunt 'had insisted upon pricking holes in the lids in the form of the constellations so that the caterpillars inside might think they were still out of doors and could see the stars' (*Diaries*, II, 19). Imprisoned in Ireland, he found consolation in watching overhead the pigeons and jackdaws, 'And once in the wind's eye, like a ship moored, / A seagull flew and I was comforted.' We learn from the same poem that he was comforted, too, by sharing his meagre fare of milk and bread with sparrows; he imagined that a spider was spinning her thread just for him, and he felt a sympathy with a 'brave mouse' who was a fellow prisoner.[9] He felt so strongly about the freedom of animals that he made his home near Cairo, around the tomb of the Moslem saint Sheykh Obeyd, a veritable paradise for them. His room was designed 'like a lantern' with windows on three sides so that he could see and hear the animals, especially at the first indication of the false dawn. Then he would dress and go to sit outside the wall of his garden to watch the sunrise and all the wild life of the desert. Two foxes within the garden filled him with delight because they came 'sometimes within a few yards of my feet, being accustomed to the work-people, and not afraid of me because I wear an Arab dress'. He gave orders that 'there shall be absolute aman ["sanctuary"] even for the wolves, and the hyenas which sometimes make their way over the garden wall'. Supervising the work, paying the wages, and pruning the trees with a pair of nippers he found 'a delightful occupation' (I, 14). His garden in the fall was 'a garden of paradise of birds and beasts ... millions of sparrows roosting nightly in the orange trees (so that the whole garden smelt in the morning like a bird-cage), everything perfection' (I, 194). He entered in his diary for April 29, 1910, that he opened his window at 3.45 that morning and that five minutes later a cuckoo began to sing. Patiently he counted the number of notes in each series of calls, the length of time between each series, and the duration of each, concluding that 'this must be a record performance. I put down the numbers on a card with a pencil while it was going on. It ended at 4.15 a.m.' And when the 'notable news' reached him of Queen Victoria's death, he was in his garden at Sheykh Obeyd, 'watching the foxes in the garden at play among the beans which were coming into flower'. Thus the short entry for January 23, 1901, was divided into an account of the pleasures of his garden and a political prophecy of 'great changes in the world' resulting from the death of Victoria. And when he had to leave Sheykh Obeyd on March 17, 1905, he sighed over its 'perpetual sunshine and its wild beasts and birds' and complained, 'Woe is me, who will look after them all when I am gone?'

It is impossible, I think, to overemphasize the importance of this trait in Blunt; at times it led him to actions and opinions amazingly Quixotic. It is difficult, for example, to sympathize completely with Blunt's feelings upon the circumstances of a tragedy in his household. In March of 1901 the standing rule at Sheykh Obeyd that even the wolves and hyenas were not to be molested resulted in a wolf's attack on an Arab kitchen helper. The boy, partly because of his father's fear of hospitals, failed to receive adequate medical treatment, suffered the physical and mental horrors of hydrophobia, and died. Blunt, of course, was full of pity for the bereaved father who had lost his son, and he was able, too, to appreciate the pathetic complaint of the father that 'I have seven daughters, anyone of which the wolf would have been welcome to, and he has taken my only son.' But he appears to have been almost equally sympathetic with the wolf who 'leaves a widow and cubs in the garden'. And he was concerned with his inability to account for the tragedy 'according to any theory of Providence, for it is not even a case of our miserable civilization being in fault'. He wondered at the time whether the disease was perhaps the result of civilization and took great pleasure in announcing when he edited his diaries for publication that according to the reports of travellers he had consulted, 'hydrophobia seems to have been introduced with other Western diseases from Europe during the nineteenth century'. By this time (1919), of course, civilization and especially nineteenth-century European civilization had become the foe in his battle against oppression.

And that battle too had its motivation in his great sympathy. When only five years old he found himself at Twyford, a school he thoroughly disliked and which he later could remember only with associations of cruelty, fear, and shame.[10] In the 'Quatrains of Life' he recalls his life at Twyford and how he used to '. . . watch the worms and beetles that have birth / Under the stones secure from outer ills' and admire them because they had the advantage of loneliness. His treasure was a snail which, though 'a creature full of fear' like himself, was yet much happier than he because it had a shell into which it could retire to escape its griefs. He kept it in a hollow bole of a tree and fed it lettuce leaves whenever he could safely escape from his schoolmates.

> And then—ah, then—who even shall tell
> The terror of that moment, when with yell
> Of triumph on their prize they broke and me
> And crushed it 'neath their heels, those hounds of Hell!
> ('Quatrains of Life')

He then consoles himself in retrospect, observing that the 'sense of justice' which God gives to man is the result of man's own suffering and that 'Man's own great need of pity . . . brims o'er / In alms to Africa and Hindostan'. One is impressed too, I think, with the way in which his boyish admiration for the snail and his mature fascination with Arabia lend themselves to comparison; Arabia he considered uncontaminated by Western civilization and he looked upon the desert as a sort of shell of protection. And while there is a certain amount of rationalization in his self-analysis of the transfer of the need for pity into a capacity for lending it, there is certainly no denying that he was deeply affected by acts of oppression all over the world. The reports of lynchings in America, and massacres of Jews in Russia or of Armenians in Turkey, all made him indignant. But it was a more intense indignation and a more personal sorrow, it seems, when the oppression and injustice occurred in the East. He wrote feverishly to the *Manchester Guardian* and to the *Tribune* about the 'abominable Denshawai affair', trying to arouse public opinion to oppose Cromer's obvious intention to impose stiff reprisals on the villagers for their attack on Englishmen. But nothing could stop the carrying out of the executions. On the day after the hangings he recorded in his diary (II, 147), 'I have worried myself all day about the Egyptian villagers, and I see now that they were hanged yesterday under circumstances of revolting barbarity. All day I have been writing, and the thing is weighing on me like a nightmare still.'

This quality of sympathy is what Blunt looked for in others. He found Herbert Spencer disappointing because the philosopher was 'so very dry, and so much wrapped up in himself, his ailments, his work and his ideas, to the exclusion, it seems to me, of individual sympathies'. He missed in him the 'softening character which old age so often gives, and which is so touching'

(I, 318-9). One suspects, too, that it is the 'softening character' which he found lacking in Henley (II, 63). For besides being repelled by what he considered the motive for Henley's attack on Stevenson (the latter's 'conversion to respectability' upon his marriage) and by his picture of Henley as one endowed with 'the bodily horror of the dwarf, with the dwarf's huge bust and head and shrunken nether limbs', he was even more unsympathetic towards him because Henley impressed him as having 'the dwarf malignity of tongue and defiant attitude towards the world at large', and especially because of 'Henley's deification of brute strength and courage, things I wholly despise'. And so he excused himself from attending Henley's funeral on the not quite truthful grounds that he never went to funerals. For when they concerned people with a touch of that 'softening character' or with a touch of physical beauty, death and funerals were the occasions for great outpourings of sympathetic comment and even for personal appearances. When Lord Stanley of Alderley died, Blunt found it 'most touching' that 'he loved nature and real sport, and Oriental learning', and that 'he had a fair estate to rule over, and he enjoyed improving it in his own way'. His 'great regard for him, indeed affection', depended in no small measure upon Stanley's profession of Islam and upon his refusal to take advantage of his right as a Moslem to put away his 'socially impossible and mad' wife because 'he never had the heart to do so' (II, 80-1). In that same year (1903) slightly over a month after he had refused to go to Henley's funeral, Blunt attended that of Lady Galloway whom he had known as a pretty girl years before. 'It was pitiful, tragic, touching, with the sunlight streaming through the windows on the Cecil monuments' and he followed the mourners to the grave 'which they had made in a sunny corner under the wall' (II, 68-9). Upon the death of Father Tyrell, a leading figure in the Modernist movement, Blunt went to view the body and though it looked 'more like an accidental handful of shapeless clay than anything that had been alive', he knelt beside the body for a time, recited a 'De Profundis' and 'kissed the hem of his garment, or rather the stole'. He left 'moved, as one could not help being moved, to tears of pity. It was so utter an ending' (II, 255). And he had 'a terrible time of depression' in 1905 climaxed by the news of the death in the desert of the pretty Bedouin Aida. She was a 'tall, straight girl with beautiful eyes and a sweet pathetic voice', and her being fatally stricken with smallpox was 'so miserable a thing' that he could not 'bear to think of it' (II, 113).

It is this same quality of pathos which Blunt found so appealing in the pre-Islamic poets of Arabia. Their 'naïvetés' were displayed in tender scenes of love, sorrowful partings, pathetic deaths, and tearful remembrances of those separated from them by death. The learned commentators in Egypt considered these to be blemishes in poetry; they admired rather the intricacies of prosody than the meaning of the images and Blunt realized that he was 'despised for admiring' the *Mu'allakat*.[11] In more impersonal things, too, he was impressed with emotional significances. He records in his 'Paris Diary of 1870' (*Diaries*, I, 390) that he attended the Opera to hear 'Masaniello' when between the third and fourth acts several patriotic songs were sung. The singing of the *Marseillaise* was especially impressive, he thought, the leading actor concluding by kneeling and draping around him the tricolour; and though the little gilt eagle on the tricolour and the military uniform on the singer tended to lessen the effect on him, he could report that he had 'seldom been so touched'. When he was sixty-three he observed that the view of Cairo as it was approached from the desert presented a dazzling contrast—a foreground of white stone quarries, the city beyond with towers, walls, and minarets stretching for miles, and 'yet further still the Nile and the Nile Valley, seven miles across and green as a spinach bowl'—and it came upon the view so suddenly as one approached the edge of the cliff which overhangs the city, that it brought tears to his eyes 'as sudden wonders are apt to do' (II, 79–80). And as in the spectacles of nature, he appreciated the emotional appeal in philosophies as well; for example, though he was quite impressed by George Bernard Shaw, his conclusion after hearing him expound his views was that 'the Fabian position has nothing to recommend it', because 'it is socialism without the few humanitarian virtues which commonly go with it, without romance and without honesty of principle, only opportunism'. Of course Blunt could not possibly have sympathized with Shaw, because Shaw was 'defending the part he had taken against the Boers in the late war' (II, 28).

But Catholicism he found very attractive. Edith Finch writes (pp. 21–2) that when the mother announced to the young Blunt children in 1847 that she had embraced Catholicism, 'the children, filled with unspeakable shame, burst into tears'. Not long afterwards, however, Wilfrid was quite happy with the Jesuits at Stonyhurst and especially with Father Porter whom he always remembered as his 'spiritual father'. He remained only six months, but was later convinced that if he had remained longer the beneficial influence would have been permanent and he 'might now [1876] have been a Jesuit'. At Oscott where he was next sent, he found the same religion 'unattractive' at first: 'the soul cried out for more; and at last it was provided' in the person of Dr. Charles Meynell who almost immediately upon his arrival became the 'intellectual father' of the young Blunt. Father Porter had 'based the truths of religion on the heart' and the emotional Blunt was happy; Dr. Meynell 'built them up to a more imposing structure in the intelligence' and this was to become the source of much difficulty.[12] Nevertheless he always looked back upon his relationship with Meynell and with Oscott with the fondest regard. He must have thought seriously of becoming a religious for in 'Quatrains of Life' he writes of this period:

> The voice that called me was a voice of good,
> It spoke of feasts less vain than the world's food,
>   And showed me my place set a quest for aye
> Of heavenly things in that calm brotherhood.

But he shrank from the voice:

> Yet thus it is. Our fallen human blood
> Is ever a mixed stream 'twixt bad and good
>   And mine, perhaps, worse mingled than the rest,
> Flowed in a baser, a more prurient flood.

'And so it might not be', and when his will 'was weaker than a child's' his 'pride stood in rebellion and said nay'.

In 1876, after about a decade of diplomatic service, an assortment of love affairs in different parts of Europe, and then seven years of marriage, he began a correspondence with his old intellectual father Dr. Meynell in an attempt to regain the faith he had loved so much at Stonyhurst and Oscott. He affirmed in that correspondence (pp. 9–10) that he had a reverence and love for the Jesuits who had educated him and no enthusiasm at all for Mill, Spencer, or Huxley, and no belief in 'the perfectibility of the human race, by means of State education in the physical science'. And yet, in spite of this temperamental alliance with Catholicism, he could not believe in Catholic doctrines. He wrote: 'I am a materialist but *"bien malgré moi"*; and my sympathy with the things of darkness is only the sympathy of despair.' Later, in 1886 when he had been politically unsuccessful and when he was 'sick alike of the affairs of the world and of the vain pursuit of happiness', he went on a pilgrimage to Rome where he thought he might perhaps 'recover my lost faith in supernatural things and end my days in piety'. He had an audience with Pope Leo XIII and was almost bewildered to find himself 'absolutely alone with one so nearly divine'. He was so impressed with the Pope's kindliness, tenderness, and personal interest that though 'he could not give me all I asked . . . when I left him it was in tears' (II, 64–5).

Quite naturally, one of the features of Catholicism which particularly repelled him was its doctrine of hell. On November 18, 1911, even though he was an old man, he could remember well 'a terrible "retreat" given at Stonyhurst, in which the physical horrors of hell were emphasized in detail'. This practice of the Jesuits, and their novitiate, 'the most mentally crushing process ever invented', were some of the things which marred his affectionate regard for them. But the affection, as well as his natural sympathy with the emotional aspects of Catholicism, motivated his several attempts to rejoin the Church and his many periods of regret at having abandoned his early faith. In 1892 he heard from Meynell about 'a new movement within the body of the English Catholic clergy', the new Modernistic movement, 'rationalistic and mystic, which embraced all forms of religion and repudiated the finality of any doctrine of the Church, a kind of positivism and creed of humanity in which Plato, and Buddha, and Mohammed were alike canonized as saints, and Christ himself hardly more than these'. He suspected, in spite of his manifest tone of delight in reporting the conversation, that it was 'altogether incredible', and in another talk with Meynell found that his first impression had been too hastily formed and that the leaders of the new movement firmly believed in 'the doctrine, fundamental and final, of the divinity of

Christ'. Nevertheless, the talk with Meynell left him in high spirits for it opened to him 'a view of a religious position, not absolutely illogical, in which I may still be loyal to all my ideas without quarrelling with the Catholic Church' (I, 75–6). A month later he advanced travel money for two of the leaders of this movement among the Capuchins, Father Cuthbert and Father Angelo de Barry, in order that they might go to Rome. He was very disappointed when they returned without having gained an audience with the Pope and with 'a flea in their ears' and very sadly accepted their honourable offer to return to him the journey money (I, 83). For at least two years before this (since 1890) he had been lamenting his defection from the Church, observing, on January 15, 1900, upon reading Mivart's article on the 'Continuity of Catholicism', that 'if, forty years ago, I had found a Catholic equally bold, I should have been saved from much infidelity, but now it is too late'. And on another occasion he declared that 'certainly, Father Tyrrel is as enlightened a priest as I have ever met. He agreed with me that it was impossible not to believe in Evolution, whatever might be pronounced at Rome.' 'Forty years ago', he wrote, 'a priest so outspoken would have saved my faith' (I, 368).

The background of sympathy develops also into the specific form of his interest in love. According to Miss Finch (p. 22), Blunt first fell in love when he was eleven; Annie Laprimaudaye was sixteen and later joined a convent in Rome. In his 'Quatrains of Life' he muses over this first love and imagines 'with later eyes of light' that there were moments when she would have welcomed more ardent attention, and he wonders

> How had it been if youth had been less weak
> And love's mute hand had found the wit to speak.
>   If thou hadst been less valiant in thy tears,
> And I had touched the heaven which was thy cheek?
>
> Would life have been to me what now it is,
> A thing of dreams half wise and half unwise,
>   A web unpatterned where each idler's hand
> Has woven his thoughts, flowers, scrolls, and butterflies?

Miss Finch reports also (pp. 30–2) that when he was eighteen he became part of London society and immediately fell in love with his cousin Mary Currie. This romance was short-lived, for in November of that year, 1858, he passed his examinations and received his nomination to the diplomatic service, and his attention turned to others. Miss Finch explains that there was some temporary difficulty that had to be overcome before Blunt was appointed unpaid attaché at the end of the year. After being nominated he unexpectedly received a letter stating that because his references were not satisfactory his nomination would not go through. His aunt, Mrs. Wyndham, immediately took her young charge in tow and called at the Foreign Office where they were confronted with Walford's charge that Blunt had made 'an attempt on his wife's virtue'. Miss Finch is sure that the charge was unfounded, but the explanation which she derives from Blunt's unpublished papers is interesting in another way: first, Blunt had been living with the Walfords the previous winter and had often taken the wife's part in the family's frequent bickerings; and second, when confronted with the unexpected charge and after being subjected to the merciless gibing of some waggish private secretaries in the outer office, the young man's 'nerve was shattered' so that he was 'completely tongue-tied and burst into tears'. If one could imagine Richard Burton faced with this situation, the contrast of the characters of these two men would need no further analysis. Burton, one suspects, either would have 'called out' the private secretaries as a preparation for dealing with Walford himself, or would have supplied them with further details in order to make the alleged crime appear more heinous.

After his appointment Blunt's love affairs became less idealistic. Miss Finch writes (p. 34) that at Athens he 'became a Byron worshipper' and began to imagine that he himself was a sort of Byronic figure—a pose perhaps fortified by the passion he had for Helen Leutwein while he carried on a lighter romance with 'the blue-eyed, barefoot daughter of Edward Noel, one of the last English Philhellenes'. Both these loves inspired verses which he set down in a black notebook. But it was in Paris, in September, 1863, that he first surrendered himself to passionate love. He met Catherine Walters, called 'Skittles' because she frequented a skittles alley where English gentlemen in Paris were wont to gather. She was perhaps one of the most famous courtesans of the late nineteenth century and she held Blunt's affection even after he ceased to be her lover. In his

'Quatrains of Life' the relationship between the experienced beloved and the ardent, though comparatively inexperienced lover is deftly portrayed—and regretted. She is Manon in the sonnet sequence 'Esther' and indeed one is tempted to conclude that Blunt was able to draw indiscriminately from both his own experiences and from Prévost. After three years in Paris he was transferred to Lisbon where he was 'very unhappy and very desirous of being happy', a time of his life which he called his 'most poetical phase'. He said, 'I was constantly expecting a letter from a person to whom I was attached, which did not come, and I consoled myself with running about the hills with some young ladies or carousing on the Peña with Don Fernando and his unmarried spouse.' [13] It was during this period that he profited from the influence of Robert Lytton who was already an established poet and who was fascinated with Blunt's 'wondrous elasticity of life', a quality which Miss Finch (p. 47) describes as 'the rare gift of communication to all who came into contact with him, a sense of life and of heightening for them the significance of even the least and most ordinary of objects, feelings, ideas'. Lytton once wrote to him, 'I long to bathe my sensations for a moment in the buoyancy of yours, as a tired traveller longs for a plunge in some fresh mountain pool.' While the younger refreshed the older poet, Lytton gave Blunt needed direction and much encouragement for writing his verses.

He looked for the sentiments of love in the literature of others too. On April 22, 1907 he claimed that the most wonderful poetry ever written was the Song of Solomon, and that he 'would sooner have written it than the whole of the rest of literature'. He could not understand how it got into the canon of Holy Scripture 'for it is pure sexual passion without the least trace of religious sentiment, all the more beautiful for that'. On January 6 of the following year he felt that the 'Love Letters of a Portuguese Nun' were 'the most beautiful ever written' and he wished he could 'be sure of their authenticity', for he would have liked 'to believe in them'. And finally, when in 1909 he had read Rousseau's 'Confessions' again after forty years he found that his opinion of the book was still the same: 'the early part, before he went to Paris and grew famous, is wonderful as a work of art and justifies itself as a young man's confession, for in spite of its crudities it is beautiful. But the rest is ugliness unredeemed.' He fancied that his own memoirs would give the same impression, 'though my youth has been prolonged beyond all measure and his ended very early'.[14]

4

Reviewing the manifestations of Blunt's temperament up to 1858, one can see emerging out of the background of sensitivity and capacity for sympathy distinct patterns of a profound pity for the oppressed, a temperamental affinity with emotional Catholicism, and an inclination towards idealistic love. Time itself would have been enough to bring these patterns into complicated relations with one another, but the process was hastened by interweaving threads of religious and philosophical doubt.

It is not surprising that this doubt also had its beginnings in his sensitiveness. At the Embassy in Athens the atmosphere was Protestant rather than Catholic and Protestant Helen Leutwein, with whom he thought he was deeply in love, died in his second year there. Miss Finch (p. 34) asserts perhaps too strongly that this event presented Blunt with the 'dilemma' that Helen being a Protestant was, 'according to his teaching, in danger of HellFire'. A rather fine point of Catholic doctrine is involved here; but since Miss Finch does not indicate the basis for her judgment and since, so far as I know, Blunt himself did not write on the problem, it is profitless to pursue the question further. But that some disarrangement of his inclinations towards Catholicism and towards love was beginning to set in at this time, there can be no doubt. While there is no difficulty in reconciling Catholicism and ideal love, it is not hard to imagine the struggle between the demands of chastity and those of the body of a sensuous youth of twenty. He himself emphasized a philosophical problem. He wrote to Meynell (pp. 25–6) that it was at Constantinople, where he stopped for some weeks on his way to take up new duties at Frankfort, where he found himself 'face to face with the first great difficulty which besets an inquiry into the rival claims of faith and reason, namely the existence of more faiths than one'. He explained also that at this time he began to find it 'in many ways irksome' to practise and profess his religion even among Catholics; 'more so than I should find it at the present day; for in early youth there are few things which a sensitive person feels more keenly than any singularity, whether it is of person or mind, or even of dress'.

But it was not until he reached Frankfort that the struggle came to a climax. It was in 1861 and all the intellectual talk was about Darwin and *The Origin of Species*. In his correspondence with Meynell (p. 27) Blunt explains that he wrote to his confessor in England asking for permission to read such things as the *Origin* and *Essays and Reviews*, for he felt he could no longer 'resist the temptation of a full indulgence in the reading I desired'. When the permission was refused, he committed his 'first deliberate sin' and was so impressed with Darwin that he became 'more than ever dissatisfied' with Catholic doctrine. He had before been merely perplexed; he was now in grave doubt, and neglected his duties as a Catholic. But he was still enough of a believer to be 'greatly frightened' at his 'state of mortal sin' and during all of that winter he was afraid to ride across country lest he break his neck and thus die in the state of mortal sin. During this time he wrote a private paper in answer to an article shown him by Count Usedom which asserted that God could be discovered in Nature. In his diary for February 10, 1906, he records with some pride that that private paper developed the germ of monistic materialism at a time before Haeckel had written anything, and in great detail he reproduces his arguments in the entry for January 19, 1909, after just reading Haeckel's Berlin lectures on evolution. The result of his splurge of reason was not satisfying: 'The Matter God I had imagined in place of the personal God was a thought that made me giddy when it presented itself first to me, as a demon by my incantations out of the forbidden books that I was reading; and in the middle of my intellectual debauch I found life unutterably sad'. He could not now return to 'that other consoling doctrine of Man's supernatural destiny, his life beyond the grave'. In the 'Quatrains of Life' there is evidence that he realized, at least in 1914, that the desire for the pleasures of love had combined with intellectual pride to shatter his faith: 'from that hidden life' at Stonyhurst and Oscott he had gone 'hungry to a world of strife, / The world of pleasure, and with heart keen set / For human joy. . . .' Two things he resolved to learn: the meaning of the physical universe and the 'power of Love'.

> What Quixote on what steed
> Of foundered folly urged to headlong speed
>   E'er chose his path more madly, or fell down
> Proner on life's least lenient stones to bleed?
>
> Striding my horse of reason with loose rein,
> I tilted at all shadows in disdain.
>   To each eternal I my question put,
> 'What art thou, for Man's pleasure or his pain?'

'War with God' was declared, it seemed to him, when he reacted to his beloved sister's intention of joining a convent by going to England and arranging that she 'put off her intention' until she should become of age. He gradually began to disbelieve in the existence of God but still was not ready to console himself 'for the loss of God and of a future life with the pleasures of the world'. His final attempt to regain his faith was the making of a retreat in the Redemptorist house at Clapham, late in the summer of 1862, but in spite of his sincere efforts, in the end he was unable to say 'I believe'; and except for a short period later when he was nursed back to health by a kind Sister of Charity, he never again believed in the doctrines of Catholicism. In the autumn of 1863 he 'fell in love, and began to lead an immoral life'. During the three years of his love for 'Skittles' his passion sufficed him, and he could not agree with Meynell that human love could never satisfy the cravings of the soul. During all that time he 'did not think of or regret the loss of religion'. But in 1867 he was again yearning for reconciliation with his lost faith and he wrote to Meynell (p. 29) that he was 'no longer satisfied with anything that the world can give'.

Meynell's letters were good, but evidently not good enough. Towards the end of the correspondence (p. 174) Blunt wrote that sometimes he thought he could believe but that his soul was weak and that 'if she could always find pleasure enough to her hand, she would be content, even now, with ignorance. The least amusement, while it lasts, shuts everything else out, and pleasure, sweet, palpable pleasure still fairly turns her head.' This is the new pattern which finally emerged out of the struggle of the 'sixties and early 'seventies. Beginning with his marriage in 1869 and his inheritance of the family estates shortly afterwards, a calm sensuousness, a hedonistic attitude, gradually replaced the passionate love and religious turmoil. His quatrains 'Sed Nos Qui Vivimus' (1888–89) strike this new tone:

> I love to touch the links of life between us, the blind kindness
>   Of joy unreasoned, solace in the sun, in shade delight
> The unhuman part of Man is still the best, his love of children,
> His love of meads and vales at home, his fondness for his kind.

And

> How beautiful is life! The present sense of souls that love us;
>   The enfolding spirit of love, made known in divers silent ways;
> The wife, the child, the man and maid, whose zeal and faith enthrone us
>   High in their temple niche enshrined! Thus angels serving stand.

Perhaps not the least of the effects of Arabic culture on Blunt was its influence in helping to bring about this transformation from the state of internal turmoil which existed before 1876. And again, it is only that basis of tremendous sympathy in his temperament which made it possible for Arabic culture to have any influence at all.

5

We know from his *Secret History*[15] that in order 'to escape a late spring in England' and because Blunt was 'in indifferent health', he and his wife in 1873 began the first of a series of journeys into the Arabic-speaking world. At Constantinople he suffered a serious attack of pneumonia, but after his recovery he bought a few pack horses from the horse market in Stamboul, took them across to Scutari and 'spent six pleasant summer weeks wandering in the hills and through the poppy fields of Asia Minor, away from beaten tracks' and keenly observing Turkish peasant life. 'We were impressed,' he wrote, 'as all travellers have been, with the honest goodness of those people and the badness of their Government.' Through interpreters they talked with the peasants and when some complained of hardships imposed by their rulers, Blunt told them that 'there were countries in still worse plight than their own, where if a poor man so much as lay down by the roadside at night and got together a few sticks to cook a meal he ran risk of being brought next day before the Cadi and cast into prison'. The listeners refused to believe that such tyranny could exist anywhere in the world, and Blunt's obvious deduction that civilization was infringing upon personal liberty was 'the earliest political reflection I can remember making in regard to Eastern things'. In the early part of 1874 the Blunts were in Algeria where they found occasion for more political reflection when they witnessed 'an Eastern people in violent subjection to a Western'. The war between Germany and France had occasioned an Arab uprising and 'the Mohammedan natives were now experiencing the extreme rigours of Christian repression'. In spite of all his love for the French, he found his sympathies wholly with the Arabs. In that same year he had some slight contact with the great tribes of the Sahara at Jebel Amour. He was delighted with 'their noble pastoral life', with 'their camel herds and horses', and their 'life of high tradition filled with the memory of heroic deeds'. On the other hand, 'the ignoble squalor of the Frank settlers, with their wineshops and their swine', raised his indignation at the 'incongruity which has made of these last the lords of the land and of those their servants'. Though he regarded it as not his personal affair, 'it was a new political lesson which I took to heart'.

In the winter of 1875-6 the Blunts, without any more serious thought 'than that of another pleasant travelling adventure in Eastern lands', paid their first visit to Egypt. They intended to become acquainted with the country districts and 'not to waste time on a city already in part European', and so came to have intimate contacts with the fellahin, the peasants, whose champion Blunt was to become. He found them in extreme poverty, being hounded by the tax collectors who had to answer the call of the European bondholders who 'were clamouring for their "coupons"'. On the market days they beheld the pitiful sight of women selling their clothes and ornaments to the Greek usurers, 'because the tax collectors were in the villages whip in hand'. The Blunts bought the trinkets and listened to their sad stories, but 'did not as yet understand, any more than did the peasants themselves, the financial pressure from Europe which was the true cause of these extreme exactions'. They laid the blame on the Egyptian authorities, 'little suspecting our English share in the blame'. In 1876 he was still 'a believer in England', and he 'shared the common idea of the beneficence of her rule in the East'. He had 'no other thought for the Egyptians than that they should share with India', which he had not yet visited, 'the privilege' of English protection.

In the spring they paid their first visit to Arabia, but the trip was insignificant and at times difficult because they were so unfamiliar with Arabic. In the winter of 1877–8, they made contact with the great Bedouin tribes of Mesopotamia and the Syrian Desert, and since they now knew something of the language and customs of the Arabs the trip was 'most interesting and successful'. It produced his wife's *Bedouin Tribes of the Euphrates*, in the writing of which Blunt had some part; it furnished Blunt with the beginning of what was to be the famous Crabbet stud; and most important of all, it developed in Blunt a sympathy for the Arabs which was to influence him for the rest of his life. In the fall of 1878 they travelled to Arabia again, hoping 'to penetrate into Central Arabia and visit Nejd, the original home and birthplace of the Arabian horse'. The result of this visit was an understanding of 'the ancient system of free government existing for so many centuries in the heart of that wonderful peninsula', and a confirmation of 'the enthusiastic feelings of love and admiration' which he 'already entertained for the Arabian race'. He called it 'a political "first love", a romance which more and more absorbed me, and determined me to do what I could to help them to preserve their precious gift of independence'. Arabia appeared to him as a 'sacred land' where he 'had found a mission in life' which he was 'bound to fulfil'. On the journey they passed through 'the civilized but less happy world of Irak and Southern Persia' which they came back to visit in the following spring. The contrast these countries provided with Central Arabia, though both were inhabited by the same Arab race, confirmed him in his conviction that the Arab world must be free from Turkish oppression. His hope was still that this could be achieved under English protection.

In 1879, at the invitation of Lord Lytton who had now been

Viceroy for over two years, the Blunts went to India. Lytton gave instructions to Sir Alfred Lyall, who was his Foreign Secretary, to give Blunt all possible information which might be helpful in the development of his 'Arabian ideas', ideas with which Lytton, 'as a man of romance and a poet', immediately 'professed his sympathy'. He received also extensive information on Indian finance. In a letter written while at Simla he complained,

> I have been studying the mysteries of Indian finance under the 'best masters', Government secretaries, commissioners, and the rest, and have come to the conclusion that if we go on *developing* the country at the present rate the inhabitants will have, sooner or later, to resort to cannibalism, for there will be nothing but each other to eat. I do not clearly understand why we English take their money from these starving Hindoos to make railroads for them which they don't want, and turnpike roads and jails and lunatic asylums and memorial buildings to Sir Bartle Frere, and why we insist upon their feeding out of their wretched handfulls of rice immense armies of policemen and magistrates and engineers. They want none of these things, and they want their rice very badly, as anybody can see by looking at their ribs. As to the debt they have been saddled with, I think it would be honester to repudiate it, at least as a debt of India. I never could see the moral obligation governments acknowledge of taxing people for the debts they, and not the people have incurred. All public debts, even in a self-governing country, are more or less dishonest, but in a foreign despotism like India they are a mere swindle.
>
> (*Secret History*, pp. 62–3.)

His brief visit to India, as he himself acknowledges, had 'considerable influence' in shaping his subsequent attitude towards British Imperialism. At this time, however, he still believed, 'but with failing faith, in the good intentions, if no longer the good results', of English Eastern rule, and thought it could be improved if only the people in England could be made aware of its shortcomings. The threads of his concern with the Arab world begin to show clearly in the pattern of his life by June 26,

1880, when he entered in his journal, 'If I can introduce a pure Arabian breed of horses into England and help to see Arabia free of the Turks, I shall not have quite lived in vain.'

At the age of forty, not only had he never taken part publicly in politics, but had 'never so much as made a speech to an audience or written an article for a review, or a letter to a newspaper'. He described himself as 'constitutionally shy in early life' and therefore reluctant to gain publicity, an attitude strengthened by his experience in diplomacy which 'always affects secrecy' whether or not it has anything to hide. Now, with 'a mission in the Oriental world, however vague and ill defined', he began to speak and write and even to appear on a platform. On August 22, 1880, he spoke at a meeting of the British Association at Sheffield opposing Captain Cameron's advocacy of a Euphrates Valley Railroad. He perhaps had in mind the lessons in finance which he had learned in India, for he raised the question of whether or not the railroad would be able to pay for itself. Already he was fighting against any kind of imposition by the West on the East. Later, in his *Secret History of the English Occupation of Egypt* (1907) he called attention to the fact that his wife was the granddaughter of Lord Byron and asserted that in view of the political events of 1881–1882 which made England virtual ruler of Egypt, both he and his wife felt 'that to champion the cause of Arabian liberty would be as worthy an endeavour as had been that for which Byron had died in 1827 [*sic*]' (p. 7). He soon saw that to be effective in his mission he had to work from within Islamic thought rather than as an outsider and he therefore took advantage of the Pilgrimage season at Jidda, seaport of Mecca, in 1881 to sit under the Ulema, or learned men. He listened and asked questions and thus gained much information about Koranic problems which later served him as an introduction to Moslem thinkers in Egypt.[16] It was at this time that England occupied Egypt and immediately Blunt's vague mission of preserving the liberty of the Arabs took on the much more specific form of agitation for Egyptian independence. He hastily wrote his first book on Eastern affairs, *The Future of Islam* (1882), in which appear the first fruits of his journeys in Arabia, Egypt, and India as well as of his questionings of Moslems at Jidda and elsewhere. For the next decade he produced a steady stream of literature on Eastern and especially Egyptian matters. Then the output began to diminish, until it finally trickled to a halt in 1912 with a few articles in *Egypt*.

His period of intense active participation in politics extended from 1881 with the beginning of the 'Egypt Question' to 1888 when he was imprisoned in Ireland and lost the Deptford election for a seat in Parliament. A survey of his particular political activities is not to our purpose, but some account should be given, I think, of the principles which guided his political activities regarding the East.

In 1882 his faith in England as the protector of weak nations had not yet been completely shattered. In *The Future of Islam* he appealed to his countrymen to remember the tremendous influence which Semitic thought had had and still had on 'the minds of nations', giving an account of the filtering of Arabian thought through France and Spain to England. 'Chivalry, a notion purely Bedouin', he hoped was 'hardly yet extinct' among Englishmen, and 'Romance, the offspring of pre-Islamic Arabia', he thought was 'still a common motive of our action', and still, 'in the rhymed verse of Yemen', a model for English poets. Englishmen still prayed 'to the God of Abraham' and revered the 'Holy Land of the Jews', that 'land which is Arabia's half-sister'. If Semitic thought is so strong in the West, how is it, he asked that we think we can overcome Islam, 'the quintessence of Arabian thought', in lands where it has flourished for centuries? 'Christendom has pretty well abandoned her hopeless task of converting Islam, as Islam has abandoned hers of conquering Europe; and it is surely time that moral sympathy should unite the two great bodies of men who believe in and worship the same God.' He reminded his readers that Islam was no less a political than a religious institution, and referred to the activities of Mohammed to prove that he founded a state as well as a religion. This is the reason, he thought, that the concessions wrested from the Ottoman Empire by the West 'failed to find acceptance anywhere with religious people'. All social and political development must conform to religious doctrine, and if the West is desirous of seeing slavery made illegal and a stricter interpretation of the Koranic permission put on marriage, concubinage, and divorce, it must allow these changes to be brought about through reform within the religion of Islam itself. He had no doubt that such points could be worked out, and hoped 'some day to have an opportunity for doing so' himself; but for the present he 'must be content with having suggested the method' for he was not in a position to 'work out the details of a reformation'.

He assured England that in spite of 'all rule written and spoken by the orthodox, that Islam cannot move', Islam was moving, and that it had failed to move temporarily only because of the unintellectual Turks who halted the progress of Arabian thought because they could not keep up with it. He claimed a liberal party had been formed in Islam corresponding to the 'Reformers' of Christianity in the fifteenth century, and he had every confidence 'that Islam, too, will work out for itself a Reformation'. The whole question was of extreme importance to England, he thought, because the problem of Moslem loyalty or revolt in India depended on it. He did not advocate English participation in the quarrel between orthodox and reformers, but suggested that 'in a perfectly legitimate way' she could 'influence the natural course of events and direct it to a channel favourable to British interests'. Moslem thinkers were becoming more and more aware that the Caliphate must retreat from Constantinople where it was under heavy pressure from forces outside Islam. Blunt's hope was to see it moved back to Arabia where it had its origin, back to Mecca where the Caliph would need 'fear no admonition from Frank ambassadors in virtue of any capitulations' and where he 'would be free to act as the Successor of the Apostle should, and would breathe the pure air of an unadulterated Islam'. Furthermore, the Caliphate at Mecca would be in a position to feel the pulse of Islam all over the world as the pilgrims streamed in to the holy shrines in season. England's role then, should be to foster this inclination to remove the Caliphate to Mecca where, as a naval power, she could secure it from all attack.

With the momentous events in Egypt in 1881 and 1882, the bombardment of Alexandria, English occupation, and the crushing of the Nationalist movement which Blunt had espoused, his noble theories of Arabian independence and Islamic reform had to give way to the pressing need for pro-Egyptian and pro-fellah propaganda. As E. M. Forster has observed,

Blunt did not 'do' much for Egypt, for in spite of his connections with the right people he never carried much weight; 'but he tried to "do" '.[17] Certainly this is of as much importance in an attempt to understand his temperament. He may have had some effect in agitating for fair treatment of Arabi, leader of the Nationalist movement, and he certainly brought to public attention details of what he considered English misrule in Egypt. As the occupation wore on and evacuation was continually put off until it became evident that there was no intention of quitting Egypt, Blunt became increasingly bitter. What little faith he had had in England's good intentions vanished; now he clearly saw British Imperialism as his real enemy and the enemy of Islam.

Cromer and his policies in Egypt became his specific target. He held him responsible for all the injustices committed and was disgusted when Cromer was given the Order of Merit after the Denshawai case.[18] In his *Atrocities in Egypt* (1906) he explained that his object in writing was to 'try and trace the history of cases' such as that of Denshawai which had happened within his recollection, and 'in this way to show the essentially inequitable basis on which the criminal relations between Englishmen and native, especially between English officer and Egyptian fellah' had been handled politically to uphold the English officer and to punish the fellah regardless of the merits of each.[19] He warned that if the Denshawai case were not taken up at the next Parliament 'in such a way as to oblige Sir Edward Grey to express his disapproval of the injustice done; if nobody in Egypt is called to account for an act of terror', he would publish the pamphlet in French, 'so that our wrongdoing may be patent to all the world', and in Arabic, 'so that every Egyptian may understand, and all the Eastern world, that British justice, so long vaunted among us, has become a vain and unmeaning word'.[20] In his conclusion he called for either an explanation from Cromer or his recall from official position in Egypt.[21] Recorded in his diary for April 11, 1907, is an account of his joy when he was awakened to receive the news that Cromer had resigned: 'I was at once full awake and laughing so that the bed shook under me, nor could I stop for several minutes. I sent back in return the single word, Whoo-whoop! I am off to Chapel Street, and Clouds tomorrow, feeling like a huntsman at the end of his day's sport with Cromer's brush in my pocket, and the mask of that ancient red fox dangling from my saddle. "Whoo-whoop!" '

But this was only a moment of joy in a long and disappointing struggle against that British Imperialism to which he traced most of the political evils of the world. In his *Secret History* (pp. 36–7) he marked as the beginning of England's departure from her traditional ways to a 'new policy of spoilation and treacherous dealing in the Levant' the 'Cyprus intrigue' and the European Congress at Berlin in 1878, from which Disraeli had returned claiming 'a public triumph' and boasting that he had secured 'peace with honour'. 'Half the crimes against Oriental and North African liberty our generation has witnessed' stemmed from this meeting. Thus he was in the same fight when he inveighed against the Italian campaign in Abyssinia in 1895 (*Diaries*, I, 207). This raid did not have 'even the excuse of calling itself a crusade' for Christendom, for the Abyssinians were themselves Christians, no less than the 'inhabitants of Calabria, while, compared with the Abyssinian Emperor who is lineally descended from the Queen of Sheba by King Solomon, the House of Savoy enthroned in the Quirinal is but a stem of yesterday'. With supreme disgust he noted on December 12, 1895, that the London Press could only comment that the campaign 'would not be "felt upon the Stock Exchange" '. When 'those blackguards of the Chartered Company in South Africa, under Doctor Jameson', raided the Transvaal and were annihilated by the Boers, he hoped 'devoutly' that Jameson who had been taken prisoner would be hanged (I, 211). He found the English papers 'sickening about the Transvaal, a mixture of swagger and poltroonery', in their making a hero out of Jameson who 'fought for thirty-six hours, and had only fifteen men killed and then surrendered, not a pretence of its being in any better cause than money-making and land-grabbing'. It was a sign of how low the English people had sunk that Austin, the new Poet Laureate, had for this occasion 'managed to turn off some spirited doggerel, and to get it recited at a music hall' (I, 214). 'The gangrene of colonial rowdyism is infecting us', he wrote on January 9, 1896, 'and the habit of repressing liberty in weak nations is endangering our own. I should be glad to see the end.' England was 'much better off and more respected in Queen Elizabeth's time, the "spacious days", when we had not a stick of territory outside the British Islands, than now, and infinitely more respectable'.

On April 30, 1891, he stopped at a place in Paris to have his hair trimmed. The barber turned out to be an ex-soldier in Tonkin, very voluble and very blood-thirsty. His philosophy was that 'en agissant avec des brutes il faut être brutal'. If he had been named Governor for only one month, 'j'aurais exterminé tout ce monde Tonquinois'. It is necessary, he said, to govern as England governs India if a nation wants to have colonies. When he asked Blunt if he agreed, Blunt replied, 'Perhaps not quite.' The 'scientific inhumanity in politics' he found distinctly on the increase because it flattered 'the selfish instincts of the strong by proving to them that their selfishness is right'. But those who tried to make an international political application of Darwin's law of the selection of the fittest 'forget that Man by the abnormal development of his reasoning powers and his invention of lethal weapons, has put himself outside the unconscious working of the natural law'. He asserted that Darwin was in no way responsible for this misapplication, because he had shown a sympathy 'with the backward races of mankind, especially in his "Voyage of the Beagle"' (I, 69–70). Nor was Blunt in sympathy with the type of patriotism which displayed itself 'in the mixed missionary and fighting language one is familiar with in Gordon's letters to his sister. These people believe they have a mission from God to establish the British flag, "the dear old Union Jack", throughout the world and to maintain it there with fire and sword. Pizzaro, no doubt, wrote in the same strain from Peru, when he destroyed the beautiful old world of the Incas. Truly "civilization is poison"'. Another type of false patriotism was that entertained by the 'commercial Imperialist', a patriot whose only concern is 'that of seizing and keeping markets' (I, 76–7). And finally, he certainly was not that kind of patriot who could feel any pride when on the Queen's eightieth birthday in 1899 *The Times* printed a 'foolish letter' which pointed out 'the wonderful fulfilment of a prophecy of Sidney Smith's who, sixty years ago, exhorted her Majesty to make it the boast of her life to avoid war and to have it on her conscience to say, "I have made no orphans or widows."' What irony 'for one whose reign has seen whole races of beings exterminated under her rule, and only the other day thanked God that her troops had destroyed 30,000 Dervishes!' [22]

Nor was he so loyal to his race that he could condone its bringing the nineteenth century to a close by 'leaving the world in a pretty pass'. The British Empire was the chief culprit only because of her wide influence; the rest of the nations of Europe and even the Americans were less guilty only because of the lack of opportunity to work havoc on the same grand scale. But they were contributing as much as they could: while English troops were burning farms under Kitchener's command in South Africa, and 'the Queen and the two Houses of Parliament, and the bench of bishops thank God publicly and vote money for the work', the United States was 'spending fifty millions a year on slaughtering the Filipinos; the king of the Belgians' had 'invested his whole fortune on the Congo, where he' was 'brutalizing the negroes to fill his pockets': and 'all the nations of Europe' were 'making the same hell on earth in China, massacring and pillaging and raping in the captured cities as outrageously as in the Middle Ages'. He commended them all equally to God's curse and bade a contemptuous goodbye to the 'famous nineteenth century into which we were so proud to have been born' (I, 375-6).

In October of 1911 he gave up his 'mission', whatever it now was, and was inclined to say with Pitt: 'Roll up the map of Islam'. By autumn of 1912, even the few articles he had been writing for the magazine *Egypt* came to an end; he gave up his London residence and spent the rest of his life as a country squire, a life 'to which I was born, and which is naturally mine'. 'Islam's chance is gone', he wrote, and 'I shall not live to see' the ultimate change which must follow the failure of the British Empire in the Mediterranean. He was sure that whatever happened, Egypt would 'never get out of the grip of Europe', and that, though Islām would survive as a religion, 'perhaps for many generations', it would never be regenerated as a political entity. He felt that his 'work of thirty years [had] been absolutely thrown away' (II, 401-3).

6

In this pattern of his 'mission' in Eastern lands no small part was played by his more personal struggle. We have seen that the

Wilfrid Scawen Blunt—Sheikh

struggle was between supernaturalism and materialism, or between an emotional attraction for Catholicism and a sensuous love of life—or, what is more likely, a combination of both which defies analysis. The struggle was solved temporarily by passionate love for 'Skittles' in the early 'sixties, but by 1876 the struggle was again raging and his correspondence with Meynell was motivated by a desire to regain his faith in Catholicism. It is not difficult, then, to make the analogy between 'Skittles' and Arabia: just as his passionate love for 'Skittles' had allayed the bitter struggle in 1863, so was the renewal of that struggle temporarily solved in 1878 by his interest in Arabia, 'a political "first love", a romance which more and more absorbed me, and determined me to do what I could to help them to preserve their precious gift of independence' (*Secret History*, p. 58). This is the background of the pattern of his concern with Islam as a religion, for it developed into a theory of returning the Caliphate to Arabia, a desire to take a personal part in the religious reformation of Islam, a desire to find a hermitage in the desert and, finally, into a permanent turning away from all religions.

We know from *The Secret History* (p. 89) that in the summer of 1880 he was 'full of the notion of going to Arabia and heading a movement for the restoration of the Arabian Caliphate. People have been called great who have sacrificed themselves for smaller objects, but in this I feel the satisfaction of knowing it to be a really worthy cause.' In the following year, as we have seen, he was at Jidda becoming acquainted with Moslem thought, and by 1882 when he published *The Future of Islam* he had convinced himself that there was the possibility of liberal reform in Islam. He explained in this book that 'the great difficulty which, as things now stand, besets reform is this: the Sheriat, or written code of law, still stands in orthodox Islam as an *unimpeachable* authority'. Though 'an excellent law', it was not entirely satisfactory on certain points; but he was reasonably certain that a 'wider and more liberal reading of the law', would result if Arabian thought once more became supreme in Islam, and that it was even possible, should that happen, that Islam and Christianity might effect a 'true reconciliation'. He believed that 'the path of Orthodox Islam is no macadamized road such as the Catholic Church of Christendom has become' and that there was no 'office corresponding even remotely with the infallible Papacy'. Tracing its history, he observed that Islam 'in its institution, and for many centuries after its birth, was eminently a rationalistic creed; and it was through reason as well as faith that it first achieved its spiritual triumphs'. He also noted that when the Arabs came in contact with Greek philosophy in the eighth century they 'assimilated it by a natural process of their reasoning into the body of their own beliefs; and now in the nineteenth they are assimilating a foreign morality into their own system of morals'. Intellectual growth of Islam, he claimed, was arrested by the Turks who, when they overran the East in the sixteenth century, found the Moslem code of Abu Hanifah a convenient form of legality and, once having gained complete authority, 'declared further learning profane, and virtually closed the schools'. Thus was reason shut out from Islam.

Whether or not this view of Islam is accurate is not here important. But it is important to note that Blunt had described the religion in a way which made it highly acceptable to himself. In its amalgam of reason and faith and in its flexibility of moral code it might well have been born of Blunt's own desire. But his political activity of the following seven years prevented him from coming any closer to embracing Islam. In 1889, after being released from prison in Ireland, he took stock of his political accomplishments. He records in his diaries (I, 25-6) that he thought he had saved Egypt from absorption by Europe, and that he had 'certainly, by stopping the Soudan war of 1885, put back the clock of African conquest for a generation, perhaps for a century'. But he despaired of 'doing good in the world in any public way'. He felt that he had 'done enough—possibly too much', and he was 'sick and weary of the machinery of public life'. And so he turned to 'the world of art and poetry' in which he felt confident he could accomplish something, and 'with an advantage of experience not every poet has'. And 'then, how delightful life is in perfect liberty!' He felt that he was never 'more capable of enjoyment, of the pleasures of friendships, of the casual incidents of romance, of the continuous happiness of life at home'. This is the mood caught in the passages of 'Sed Nos Qui Vivimus' which are quoted above. He was quite happy. He found that his prison experience had not discredited him with his 'women friends', but rather that it was a 'title to romantic interest' which made it easy for him to take up again his place in society. This and the paternal interest in his growing daughter kept his mind free from politics for the next few years.[23] When he was at his winter home in Egypt, he occupied himself with improving his property. He wrote at this time (I, 15), 'I could be quite content to spend the rest of my days in this pleasant work.'

But on October 26, 1894, he was noting in his diary that he and his cousin Terence Bourke 'had made a plan of going in the Spring to visit the Senussi in the Tripolitan desert and perhaps making profession of Islam'; and 'I think a hermitage of the kind I have been seeking might be found in the country near Cyrene'. Though the plan did not work out and the hermitage near Cyrene was forgotten, at the end of January in 1896 he was again thinking the same thoughts. He felt that the future for him was dark; he wrote: 'If this next summer brings me nothing of value to my life I shall not return to England again. Perhaps I may find my heritage this Spring in truth and reality.'

But it was not until the *next* Spring, in 1897, that he started for Benghazi and Siwah full of enthusiasm and regretting only that Lady Anne was not going with him. Beseys, his Arab companion, listened to his wish for a hermit's life in the desert and promised to take him to his own spiritual father, Sidi Maymum, who was living that kind of life in the Jebel Akhdar. They talked so earnestly on these matters that they lost their way 'and were some time finding it again'. When they came to the Senussi monastery at Zeytoun, Blunt was impressed by the brothers; 'One might do worse in the world than be a Senussi brother,' he wrote. But on the next day, February 28, 1897, began the great disillusionment. Blunt and his party were attacked and plundered by the Siwans and taken prisoners. He was roughly treated until he whispered to the Maown and some of the principal sheikhs that he was an Englishman; and though he tried to make excuses for the attack, the best of which was that it was the season of the Ramadan and 'the Siwans are mad with it', he had lost his faith in the Senussi branch of Islam. What was particularly ironic was that there was strong suspicion that the Akhwan, the monks themselves, had taken part in the attack. The attack upset the plans for going on to Jebel Akhdar, and so he never did find his hermitage. What is more, he now felt that the Senussi was not of much worth and that in the oasis towns it was 'mere madness and ought to be suppressed'. When he got back to Cairo and Sheykh Obeyd after a very hard journey he wrote his final opinion of the matter: 'My experience of the Senussi at Siwah has convinced me that there is *no* hope anywhere to be found in Islam. I had made myself a romance about these reformers, but I see that it has no substantial basis, and I shall never go farther now than I am in the Mohammedan direction. The less religion in the world, perhaps, after all, the better' (I, 276).

After political disappointment in 1888 and 1889, Blunt had turned to society and literature; now, in 1897, disappointed in his high hopes of reforming Islam and of perhaps leading the life of a hermit in the desert, he again turned to society. But his health was poor, and the rigours of his many journeys began to take their toll. No more journeys were made, all strenuous activities came to an end, and for two years he was in severe pain and near death. And yet, the threads of the former pattern of his life were still visible. On June 27, 1897, he recorded in his diary some details of a pleasant afternoon spent in talk with Alfred Austin, Lady Paget, and Lady Windsor out on a lawn at Swinford. Someone suggested that each should describe his idea of heaven and Blunt's was 'to be laid out to sleep in a garden, with running water near, and so to sleep for a hundred thousand years, then to be woke by a bird singing, and to call out to the person one loved best, "Are you there?" and for her to answer, "Yes, are you?" and so to turn around and go to sleep again for another hundred thousand years'. Depending upon juxtaposition alone to show his disgust, he set down Austin's idea: 'to sit also in a garden, and while he sat to receive constant telegrams announcing alternately a British victory by sea, and a British victory by land'.

And while he was disappointed in religion, his illness as well as his romantic inclination persuaded him to make a trip to St. Winifred's well at Holywell. 'I suppose no pilgrim ever washed there with less Christian faith and at the same time with so little of the mocking spirit,' he wrote (I, 292-3), 'I have a belief in holy places and holy people quite apart from all religious creeds and I felt a great confidence in the Saint that she would do me good.' On the day after bathing in the well he reported that he had no pain at all, 'thanks to St. Winifred'. While asserting again that he had no faith in a future existence but that of a 'dreamless sleep', he claimed St. Winifred as his patron saint because he believed in her and because he was named after his great-grandmother, Winifred Scawen. But in his 1919 comment on the passage he remembered that the cure did not last long and that no sooner had he turned his back on St. Winifred's Well than he again felt the pains. Almost at the point of death he wrote, 'The world is only meant for those who are in health, and the maxim of our forefathers was a sound one, that a dying man should keep wholly out of sight.' Then came the crisis of his illness, and when his life was spared he 'recognized that St. Winifred had only deferred her benefits, and that, as in the case of most miracles, she had chosen a natural road of cure'. In a spirit of thanksgiving he returned to Holywell, deposited there his crutches 'bound up with a nightgown' and affixed a label: 'Set here in thankful token of a cure from long sickness after bathing in St. Winifred's Well. By her servant W. S. B. October 19, 1898.' As a more practical gesture he donated £20 towards legal expenses to oppose the Town Council's intention of closing the well in order to lease it to a 'Soda Water Company'. In his thanksgiving he showed no partiality to Catholicism, however, for a few years later when he was at Sheykh Obeyd for the last time he paid a sentimental visit to the tomb where Salem, his Egyptian servant, had been saying prayers for him ever since the English sheikh had become ill. Blunt was very much impressed and he showed his gratitude to the Moslem saint by reciting a *fatha*.[24]

There were traces, too, of his early fascination with Catholicism and his embracing of reason; sitting for his portrait to Watts on March 11, 1899, he applauded the artist's description of ceremony in religion as corresponding to outline in a picture: not existing in nature, but necessary for our understanding. He liked also his explanation of the place of reason in religion, likening it to the thumb of the hand without which the fingers (sentiment, faith, charity, hope) could grasp nothing. But perhaps the applause was more excited by his aesthetic satisfaction with the images than by anything else. A few months later he was happy to learn from Mohammed Abdu that the *Hawadith*, or traditions, commanded kindness to animals, but he saw that the learned Moslem had no more faith in Islam than he himself had in the Catholic Church, and that they both envisaged 'no good future for the human race' (I, 346). At a social gathering on September 5, 1904, when he was asked whether he believed in anything supernatural he answered, 'Yes, I have a small belief in the evil eye.' At about the same time he was disagreeing with Tolstoy's ideas in so far as they indicated that the world was 'improving in the direction of justice' and 'that religion of any kind makes people unselfish' (II, 106). And in 1911, in the light of the 'Italian atrocities', he was ready to say 'To Hell with the Pope', when he heard it rumoured that the Pope was supporting Italy's declaration that the war was a crusade. Still, he thought, 'good may yet come out of this monstrous evil, for there will be a revulsion of feeling, and the world will see how hideous Christianity has become divorced from its beliefs, a mere religion of rapine' (II, 369). This was the climax of his anti-imperialism which had its start in his sympathy with the Turkish peasants in Asia Minor and the fellahin in Egypt, and in admiration for the liberty-loving Arab tribes of the peninsula.

Together with this turning away from formal religions is his glorification of the Negro race. On August 8, 1899, he had gone to London to see the 'Savage South African Show' which he called 'a return to the shows of Imperial Rome'. But the show had an effect on Blunt contrary to its purpose, for he felt only admiration for the captive 'black men' who 'managed to preserve their dignity' and make the 'white swaggerers' look foolish. 'The superiority of the black man over the white was throughout conspicuous,' he wrote, 'and it did not need the patter of the whites on the stage to explain that it was only their maxim guns that gave the latter their victory.' A dozen years later, February 21, 1911, he went to a prize fight between 'a black man and a white man'. He felt it interesting only because 'it involved a question of race superiority', and much to his surprise he found that it was the white man who was big and burly and the black who was small. But despite the disadvantage of size the Negro, Blunt was pleased to see, wore down the white fighter 'by superior science and superior courage', scoring a victory at the end of the fifth round. In considering his pleasure over the outcome, I think it is important to note not only his admiration for the Negro, but his disdain for the white man. For, about three years later in his 'Quatrains of Life' he '... dreams a dream of our fair mother Earth / In her first beauty, ere mankind had birth'. And into this paradise of Nature, not at all a Nature 'red in tooth and claw', came man:

> Among the forms of dignity and awe
> It moved a ribald in the world of law,
>   In the world's cleanness it alone unclean,
> With hairless buttocks and prognathous jaw.

These cannot be considered careless words coming as they do from a man so polite and urbane; Blunt had become misanthropic, but it was a misanthropy applied primarily to civilization, and especially to European and Christian civilization.

Despite the fact that on his seventieth birthday (August 17, 1910) he could 'pride himself' that he 'was able with ... one cup and ball to catch it on the point nine times out of twelve', age and disappointment were taking their toll. In his diaries he closed the year 1913 with the lament; 'I am alone just now here and in this dark world I am overwhelmed with woe.' Though he was still convinced of the 'soundness' of his 'view of things and of some skill and courage in expounding it', he was discouraged that he had made no converts to continue his teaching after he was dead. He thought his ideas were beginning to bear fruit in the East and that they would 'one day be justified in act', but he was wounded 'with a sense of failure' for having 'founded no personal school where my name has authority'. And most of all he 'despised' himself for minding it so much.

His permanent place as a poet he linked with the fate of the 'Eastern Nations'. He believed that if they achieved their independence from Europe he would be hailed by posterity as a 'forerunner of their cause' (II, 203-4). Most of the Eastern nations are now free from European domination; but despite Blunt's espousal of this 'cause' his fame as a poet rests on his love poetry, not on his political verse. *The Love Sonnets of Proteus* and *Esther* are perhaps his best volumes, but even in these he never reaches the heights of great poetry. He had a facility of expression, and the sincerity of his emotions makes his verse warm and intimately appealing; but the inspiration which the poet must have felt seldom comes through to the reader. And his poetry as a whole shows no marked curve of development; there is no growth of artistry. He had the poetic temperament but lacked the spark of genius. After 1917 he hardly ever left Sussex, the love of which, he said, 'is still with me the most permanent instinct of my heart'. He was almost jealous of it, resenting 'the intrusion of outside praisers of its loveliness'. Thus, wrote Miss Finch, he even 'resented *The Petworth Posy*, a small volume in which, with Kipling, Belloc, and Francis Thompson, he figured among the poets of Sussex', for he felt that only he among them was born there or had had any family connection with it. He even 'grumbled absurdly' that he resented the Roman remains which had 'no business to be here, outlandish, imperialistic'.[25] In the end he claimed that 'happiness depended on two things with me, being out of pain and being with those I loved, but ... all we can really affirm is that the natural world is on the whole a happy world and that man is a disturber in it with his tiresome intelligence and that death is the best ending for it after all'.[26]

Perhaps he made a final attempt to breach the gap between the dictates of his intellect and those of his heart when he sat down to write his *Religion of Happiness*. But it was never finished, probably, wrote Miss Finch, because 'it led him to the conclusion that "all this about the 'Aspects' of God is the veriest nonsense, as too is the whole scheme of Christianity"—a view from which he probably never again departed'.[27] Some of his friends, she wrote, claimed 'that at the last moment he regained a faith he had never really lost, in the Roman Catholic Church and its doctrines'.[28] He did receive the last rites of the Church, but it is useless to argue whether or not it was a sincere return to Catholicism; as for the Blunt we are concerned with, the pattern of his life was complete long before they wrapped him in his 'old Eastern travelling carpet' and buried him without a casket in the woods at Newbuildings.

R. B. Cunninghame Graham has said that Blunt was 'a man who touched life at a hundred different points'.[29] The truth of this statement might be confirmed even by exclusive reference to criticisms of Blunt which attempt to capture within a few words the spirit which animated a remarkable life of eighty-two years; for each attempt revolves about one of the 'hundred different points' [30]—and there are yet many points to consider. One of these is Blunt's fascination with Arabic culture.

7

We have tried to indicate that the background for an analysis of Blunt's temperament is his tremendous capacity for sympathy. It made him compassionate towards Eastern peoples suffering oppression, and this, by contrast, heightened his admiration for the free and freedom-loving Arabs of the great desert. This 'softening character' of sympathy is found too in his life as a country squire, for his rule of the Crabbet estates was gentle and paternal.[31] But he also had a squirish pride of position and antipathy towards physical labour, and these qualities helped to condition him for an admiration of the Arabs who lived under the tribal system headed by the sheikh; he dressed like one, spoke Bedouin Arabic, and followed Bedouin customs in his forty-acre oasis at Sheykh Obeyd, where he ruled over some hundred natives, many of them Bedouins from Arabia.

And the impact of Arabic culture is evident in Blunt as a poet. He admired Arabic poetry of pre-Islamic times because it was naïve in its display of emotion, uninhibited, and hedonistic. Not a remarkable linguist,[32] he depended on his wife's superior ability and he turned into verse her translations of the *Mu'allakat* and *The Stealing of the Mare*. But the life of a poet was not enough to satisfy him even before he came in contact with Arabia. He was searching, perhaps unconsciously, for a 'mission' in life, and he found it in an espousal of the cause of Arabian liberty, a vague and undefined mission at first, as he himself realized.

We have seen, too, that his struggle between a sensuous love of life and an emotional attraction for Catholicism, and its more specific corollary, his belief in the incompatibility of faith and reason, were in large measure the result of his sympathy and sensitiveness. His mission in the East served at first to allay the throes of that struggle, just as his love for 'Skittles' had superseded his religious doubts in the early 'sixties. The political crusade led him into a study of Islam as a religion, and he found it attractive partly because he conceived of it as capable of combining faith and reason. He came almost to the point of formally embracing the faith of Islam, went out into the desert to seek a hermitage, and was sadly disappointed in his hope of playing a personal role in its religious reformation.

But though it fell short of fruition, the romance lived on.[33] He had become interested in Arabic culture quite by accident when he travelled for his health at the age of thirty-five, but the circumstances of his contact with it were such that the seat of that culture, Arabia, was a 'political "first love" '. And like most first loves it grew in romantic charm in spite of, or perhaps because of, the fact that it never completely satisfied the lover.

IV

Charles Montagu Doughty— Nasrâny

I

WILFRID BLUNT dedicated *The Stealing of the Mare* 'To Charles Doughty, Esq., in recognition of His Knowledge, the most complete among Englishmen, of Arabian things'. Blunt had travelled in the area described in Doughty's *Arabia Deserta*, especially in Nejd, and he felt qualified to pass judgment on the book's accuracy. He wrote in his diary for April 26, 1888, that he was reading Doughty's book on Arabia 'which is by far the best ever written'. He found it 'exhaustive and accurate, though less sympathetic with Arabian ideas' than he expected, and he felt that Doughty saw 'the worse rather than the better nature of the people'.[1] He liked to claim that he was among the first to recognize the merits of *Arabia Deserta*, and that he introduced it to Burne-Jones and William Morris.[2] And his appreciation was more than merely aesthetic: in 1897, after having been attacked by the Senussi at Siwah, he noted in his diary that through all the difficult time he had been reading Doughty, 'certainly the best prose written in the last two centuries'. 'He is of excellent counsel,' he wrote, 'for such as we have been in; and I think it was in great measure due to his influence that I took the passive line I did the day of the attack. Any other would have cost me my life.'[3] He never lost his enthusiasm for the book and it is reported that in his later years he used to remark that he would rather have written *Arabia Deserta* than any other book of the nineteenth century.[4] But just as he considered Doughty's prose the best of the nineteenth century, so he deemed Doughty's poetry the worst.[5]

Richard Burton did not live long enough to evaluate Doughty's poetry, but he wrote a scathing review of *Arabia Deserta* upon its publication in 1888.[6] He feared that '*Mega Vivlion Mega Kakon*' would be the 'verdict of the general reader', and that while the book must be important to students of geography, epigraphy, and Arabic, yet even these must wonder at Doughty's 'worldly unwisdom'. He described the book more specifically as a 'twice-told tale writ large . . . which, despite its affectations and eccentricities, its prejudices and misjudgments, is right well told'. The account which he then gives of Doughty's errors in matters of Arabic culture and language is impressive, attesting equally to Burton's superior knowledge and to his pique at having been ignored. 'Mr. Doughty informed me', he wrote, 'that he has not read what I have written upon Arabia; and this I regret more for his sake than for my own. My "Pilgrimage" would have saved him many an inaccuracy.' Especially revolting to Burton was 'the recital of his [Doughty's] indignities' which 'at length palls upon the mental palate'. He felt that it was Doughty's ignorance of Eastern matters which caused his difficulties among the Arabs, and he recounted the ignominies: Doughty 'is bullied, threatened, and reviled; he is stoned by the children and hustled by the very slaves; his beard is plucked, he is pommelled with fist and stick, his life is everywhere in danger, he must go armed, not with the manly sword and dagger, but with a pen-knife and a secret revolver'. Nothing could be more disgusting to the proud Burton: 'Mr. Doughty assures us,' he wrote, 'that his truth and honesty were universally acknowledged by his wild hosts; yet I cannot, for the life of me, see how the honoured name of England can gain aught by the travel of an Englishman who at all times and in all places is compelled to stand the buffet from knaves that smell of sweat.'

Besides reinforcing our impressions of Blunt and Burton, these opposite criticisms point out three approaches to *Arabia Deserta*: Doughty's knowledge of the Arabs, his personal relations with them, and his prose style. The last is not so important to our purpose as are the other two; but we may take notice of the appropriateness of the style without making a stylistic analysis as such.

2

Doughty was born on August 19, 1843, and named for his father, Rev. Charles Montagu Doughty, Squire of Theberton, Suffolk.[7] His mother was the former Frederica Beaumont, daughter of the Honourable and Reverend Frederick Hotham, Rector of Dennington, Prebendary of Rochester, and son of the second Baron Hotham. From both sides he came from landed gentry. In his mother's family had been prelates, courtiers, warriors, and ambassadors, and since the middle of the seventeenth century it had produced six admirals, three general officers, a bishop, a judge, and a colonial governor. The atmosphere he was born into was thus one of aristocracy and conservatism which took for granted unquestioning loyalty and patriotism.

The baby's health was so poor that he was immediately baptized by his father. Ill health proved to be the cause of Doughty's first great disappointment. He inherited the Hothams' love for adventure and especially adventure on the sea and was trained for a career in the Navy; but he failed to pass the medical examinations in 1862. He later wrote that his life since that time had been devoted to serving his country in whatever way he could, but his disappointment lasted even to his old age; for in 1922, in a letter to Hogarth, he indicated a wistful envy of even a war-time title of Temporary Commander.

Thwarted in his first ambition, he turned to an early interest in geology with new vigour. He devoted himself to the study of Suffolk chalk and by 1862 he was able to communicate on the subject of flint implements from Hoxne with the British Association meeting at Cambridge. He was in residence at Cambridge from 1861 until 1863 when he joined several other Caius College men in a change to Downing. He took up life membership with the British Association, and in the same year, 1863, went to Norway to study glaciers. He reported to the Association at Bath in 1864 and contributed to the thirty-fourth report in the *Proceedings of the British Association*, 1866. In fuller form the article was published in a pamphlet, *On the Joestedal-brae Glaciers in Norway*, in the same year.

At Downing, he lived 'an absorbed, aloof, self-contained life'. Hogarth quotes a letter written to Doughty by the Rev. Hardinge in 1864 in which allusion is made to 'researches and noble ambition as regards this earth', and in which he approves Doughty's desire to 'soar above the vanities of this world and take a place among the worthies who have lived for its adornment and the real glory of God'. He took the Natural Science Tripos examination in December 1865, placing second in the second class. Hogarth reports that one of Doughty's examiners, T. G. Bonney, teacher in geology, said much later that he 'was sorry not to be able to give him a first, as he had such a dishevelled mind. If you asked him for a collar he upset his whole wardrobe at your feet.'

From 1865 until 1870 he studied both at London and at the Bodleian Library at Oxford, not geology or the natural sciences, but early English literature. In a statement to the *Syndics* of the Cambridge University Press in 1905 he wrote that in 1865 he had begun to think about writing 'a patriotic work (and wherein Roman, Celtic, and German *Origines* are treated of)'. And in 1923 he wrote to Hogarth that he had spent 'nearly sixty years indeed in all' in the study of the 'tradition of noble Chaucer and beloved Spenser'. At some time between 1866 and 1870 another change occurred in his life: his family suffered heavy financial losses and he became, in Hogarth's words, 'a necessitous man'.

During his reading he had become interested in Erasmus and Joseph Scaliger. It was out of a reverence for their memory, he wrote much later, that he set out for Holland and studied 'Hollandish—which with Danish (I was nearly a year in Norway in 63–4) gave me a philological feeling in English'. From 1870 to the beginning of his Arabian adventure he was a travelling student of the world. He lived modestly and alone, studying languages, history, archaeology, and geography. He spent the winter of 1870–1 in Holland and the following summer at Louvain in Belgium where he found the town 'very filthy and unwholesome' and the 'people very papistical'. Then he passed into France, working his way southwards until he found a suitable lodging on the Italian Riviera at Mentone. Here he spent the winter of 1871–2. In February he began moving south again making a tour of Italy. He lingered at Florence but spent very little time at Rome. He lived at La Cava in the private house of

Charles Montagu Doughty—Nasrâny

a Signor Cavaliere whose family served Doughty's domestic needs very well. By the end of the summer he was travelling southwards again, sailing into Messina early in September, 1872. He spent only six weeks in Sicily and three weeks at Malta. In the latter part of October he was in Algeria where he got his first glimpse of Islam and the desert and where his interest in geology was renewed. In the second week of December he was in Spain. His ill health and the difficult travelling conditions are indicated in his journals quoted by Hogarth. Barcelona was 'the only cheerful 'place he saw in Spain. From April 1873 until February 1874 he travelled in Greece. It seems that he had intended to travel in Italy, Sicily, Spain, and Greece as the Mediterranean part of his studious journeys; Malta, Tunisia and Algeria perhaps were included accidentally when he could find no easier way of travelling from Sicily to Spain.

But after the winter of 1873-4 Doughty deliberately turned his back on the West and moved into the lands of the Bible. He travelled about Syria, Lebanon, and Palestine and then into Egypt. He spent perhaps about three months on the Sinai peninsula beginning in February, 1875. Then there was a desert trip up through the peninsula out to Petra, which seems to have been the final stop in his intended Eastern travels: 'I had no other intention', he wrote in a letter to A. Sprenger, 'than to see Petra, I could speak very little Arabic . . . not having before studied the history of those countries.' On his way to Petra, Doughty camped during the night with some Arabs at a watering place called Ayn Mussa. Here he heard the Arabs talk about a place along the route of the pilgrimage to Mecca and Medina called Medáin Sâlih where there were inscriptions and monuments of stone. The next day at Petra, he again heard of the carved stones at Medáin Sâlih and he decided to be the first to see and record them for European scholars.

What followed this decision is recorded in *Arabia Deserta*. Taking on the name of Khalîl because its sound was similar to 'Carl', or 'Charles', he travelled with the pilgrimage to Medáin Sâlih, intending to join it again as it returned from the holy cities to Damascus. But after taking impressions of the inscriptions, he gave the results of his labours to a returning pilgrim asking him to leave them with the British Consul at Damascus, and he himself wandered over northwestern Arabia living both in the towns and in the desert wastes with the nomads, enduring privations and dangers and finally making his way to Jidda and thence to Bombay where after a short recuperation he embarked for England. Dressed as a Syrian, Khalîl started from Damascus on November 10, 1876; he reached Bombay in October, 1878.

There was some difficulty in arranging for the publication of scientific data which he had gathered in his travels. Professor Alois Sprenger offered to make German periodical space available to him and articles appeared in *Globus* in 1881 and 1882. These articles were necessary to establish Doughty's priority of discovery. He knew that the Blunts had reached Hayil in Nejd about six months after his own departure from Arabia, and Sprenger had told him in November, 1879, that Burton, who was about to go again to Midian, was asking questions of von Kremer about Medáin Sâlih. After much correspondence and bargaining, Doughty's impressions of the inscriptions at Medâin Sâlih were published under the direction of Ernest Renan as a separate volume of a corpus of Semitic inscriptions which was being prepared by the Paris Académie des Inscriptions. The volume, *Documents épigraphiques recueillis dans le nord de l'Arabie*, was published in 1884. Doughty felt that he had discharged his patriotic duty in this matter by first offering the British Museum the opportunity to buy his impressions: they had been 'refused rather contemptuously by Dr. Birch', he wrote to Hogarth.

Meanwhile he was hard at work composing *Arabia Deserta*, which was finally published, not without much difficulty and eventually at a loss to the publishers, by the Cambridge University Press in 1888. The difficulty in finding a publisher was the result not of the subject matter, of course, but rather of the style. But Doughty was adamant in his refusal to allow any editing of his prose. His style, usually described as archaic, is splendidly analysed by Barker Fairley and Anne Treneer. Over and above the use of Arabic words, there is a reflection in it of Arabic influence on Doughty. But in the main, Doughty's prose was evolved from his study of early English authors, and especially Chaucer and Spenser.

Barker Fairley writes that from the publication of *Arabia Deserta*, 'the story of Doughty's life would appear to be very nearly the story of his books'.[8] All these were books of verse; the only prose besides *Arabia Deserta* was a review of Hogarth's *Penetration of Arabia*, printed in *The London Observer*, March 19, 1922. This review occasioned some reminiscences of his experiences in Arabia and contains some descriptions of the desert. *Under Arms*, printed in 1900 by the Army and Navy Stores at Doughty's expense, consists of some eighty short stanzas of unrhymed octosyllabic verse. It chronicles the Boer War up to that time and urges English soldiers on to patriotic effort. In 1906 *The Dawn in Britain* was published in two volumes. Doughty had been working on his great epic since the publication of *Arabia Deserta* and thinking about it, as we have indicated, since as early as 1865. The poem, in twenty-four books, covers a space of about five hundred years in portraying the dawn of Christianity and a consciousness of nationality in 'The Utmost Isle', the planned title of the epic. In 1908 appeared his *Adam Cast Forth (A Sacred Drama in Five Songs)* based on the Moslem legend that when Adam and Eve were cast out of the garden of Eden they were separated on the earth and met afterwards at a mountain near Mecca called by the Arabs 'Arafat', or 'the recognition'. In 1909 Doughty turned to the present with *The Cliffs (A Drama of the Times, in Five Parts)*. This poem and *The Clouds* (1912) were addressed to his countrymen in an attempt to awaken them to the dangers of foreign invasion. In a letter to Edward Garnett dated January 20, 1921, Doughty wrote:

> To my mind and humble reading of Nature, a Nation without some fervent Patriotism, without Religion; that is lacking those aspirations and higher ideals which lift men above themselves: is already self-slain. It is a decadent mass of men. The Future belongs to those Communities in whom the qualities are dominant, which swell and sanctify the souls of their best sons; that thrust them on and with them *impell* the body of the People as a Tide towards the best that human nature can attain to.[9]

Such was his motivation for the two poems concerned with the present—poems which were considered jingoistic and hysterical by the audience he addressed. *The Titans (Subdued to the Service of Man)* was published in 1916, and *Mansoul or The Riddle of the*

World in 1919. In 1923 a 'new and revised edition' of *Mansoul* appeared. The poem goes beyond the historical origins of mankind into the realm of philosophic speculation on the meaning of life itself. Doughty wrote to T. E. Lawrence in 1923, 'The *Mansoul* volume has not any predecessors that I know of, since it is taken solely from Nature seen through the eyes of Chaucer and Spencer and a life's (patriotic) study of Mother Tongue. I am content to leave it a legacy to a future generation.' And in the same year, in a letter to Edward Garnett, he wrote, 'A single line of Spenser excepted, it [*Mansoul*] derives nothing that I know of, from any former books. It was the devoted work of nine late years of my Life, and is my best work.' [10]

A future generation has not yet come forth to claim the legacy of *Mansoul*, and indeed, despite the scholarly efforts of a small group of critics, notably Barker Fairley and Anne Treneer, Doughty's poetry as a whole is still unappreciated.[11] The influence of the East on his poetry is slight.[12] There are descriptive passages which harken back to *Arabia Deserta* and there is the Arafat myth in *Adam Cast Forth*; but for the most part, the impressions of primitive life and primitive desolate landscapes are the sole contributions of his experience in the East to his poetry. Doughty is still best known as the author of *Arabia Deserta* and in this book is sufficient evidence of the effect of the East on his sensibility.

3

T. E. Lawrence called *Arabia Deserta* 'the first and indispensable work upon the Arabs of the desert' and believed that 'every student of Arabia wants a copy'.[13] There is no doubt that Doughty intended to describe his experiences accurately. 'The book is not milk for babes,' he wrote in the preface to the first edition, 'it might be likened to a mirror, wherein is set forth faithfully some parcel of the soil of Arabia smelling of *sámn* and camels.' The conversations of the Arabs recorded in the book were 'written all day from their mouths' and he trusted that if they were 'rehearsed to them in Arabic, there might every one, whose life is remembered therein, hear, as it were, his proper voice; and many a rude by-stander, smiting his thigh, should bear witness and cry "*Ah Wellah*, the sooth indeed!" ' (I, 29).

Charles Montagu Doughty—Nasrâny

In many ways he was qualified to accomplish his purpose. The romantic attraction of the East has often distracted Western writers and affected their judgments on Eastern matters. And as Fairley has pointed out, 'Arabia of all countries has been the happy hunting-ground of romantic poets. It has become the chosen land of exotic romance.' He maintains that this was not Doughty's view of Arabia: 'for him Arabia had not and could never have the faintest tincture of the picturesque, because he did not approach it with that part of his nature in which the picturesque could exist.' He thinks that Doughty was concerned with 'the older channels of English life', and that his interest in Arabia was primarily historical. 'He never saw it', he writes, 'as exotic writers do, a land of dream.' [14] Rather it was a world of facts which were awaiting investigation. He had a scientific bent of mind with a scientist's respect for natural phenomena and accurate details.[15] His major interest at the University had been geology, and one of the reasons for his journey into Arabia was the hope of discovering geological and geographical data which would be of importance to European scholars. 'Of surpassing interest to those many minds, which seek after philosophical knowledge and instruction,' he wrote in the preface to the second edition of his book, 'is the Story of the Earth, Her manifold living creatures, the human generations and Her ancient rocks.' In his introduction to the book, Lawrence was explicit on the scientific nature of *Arabia Deserta* (though he did not hold that it was the only significance of the book) claiming that it 'became a military text-book, and helped to guide us to victory in the East' during the first World War. Doughty certainly did not foresee this use of his book, but he insisted on its unromantic view of Arabia. 'As for me who write,' he explained (I, 95), 'I pray that nothing be looked for in this book but the seeing of an hungry man and the telling of a most weary man; for the rest the sun made me an Arab, but never warped me to Orientalism.' And Lawrence read *Arabia Deserta* in that light: 'There is no sentiment,' he wrote, 'nothing merely picturesque, that most common failing of oriental travel-books.'

At the beginning of his journey with the pilgrimage caravan there was every opportunity to serve romanticism by indulging in description of the very colourful gathering together of the various pilgrims and their equipment. Doughty records details painstakingly, but he is inclined to obscure the romantic effects of the scene because of his dislike of 'European orientalism'.[16] The rich pageantry of the beginning of the great pilgrimage from Damascus he grudgingly and perhaps unconsciously presents to the reader (I, 105): 'Upon the bearing harness of the Takht camels are shields of scarlet, full of mirrors, with crests of ostrich plumes, and beset with ranks of little bells, which at each slow camel's foot-fall jingle, sinking together, with a strange solemnity: it is the sound of the Haj religion wonderfully quaint and very little grateful in my hearing.'

He found that 'those loose "Arabian tales" of the great border-cities, were but profane ninnery' to the 'stern natural judgments' of the nomads. But he had to admit that the nomads had so much 'of the Semitic Oriental vein, without the doting citizen fantasy, that many dream all their lives of hidden treasures; wealth that may fall to them upon a day out of the lap of heaven'. In place of the 'cities' taling' the nomad 'Aarab have their braying rhapsodies, which may be heard in every wild nomad hamlet'. They quote 'the rhythms between wisdom and mirth of the Kasasîd (riming desert poets without letters)' in telling of their past raids and adventures in the desert. But he could hardly distinguish what the *kassâd* was reciting and he found it 'a strange language' (I, 105). When he did come in contact with Oriental tales as we know them he observed that the nomads listened only with weariness. But the people of the towns found great solace in them, 'as the public plays are pleasant hours of abandonment to the citizens of Europe'. He noted that 'the matter is most what that which was heart's joy to the good old knight in the noble English poet, "*When any man hath been in poor estate and climbeth up and wexeth fortunate*" '. But in spite of their resemblance in subject matter to his beloved Chaucer, he felt that 'their long process grows in European ears (for tediousness) to be a confused babble of sounds', and he describes the tales in terms of the teller, 'Abdullah's brain-sick matter' (II, 150–1). He also dispels (I, 607) the romantic notion of the Arab singing girl. 'I never heard a woman sing,' he writes, '(other than the girls' festival chanting of single staves) in these countries.—Where be the Aphrodisiastic modulations of the fair singing women in these Arabian

Charles Montagu Doughty—Nasrâny

deserts of "the Time of Ignorance"? The harem sing not in their new Arabian austerity of a masculine religion.'

The significance of this last quotation is not immediately evident; Doughty is intimating neither an attraction for 'Aphrodisiastic modulations' nor sympathy with the 'new Arabian austerity of a masculine religion'. Least of all is it merely an accurate recording of fact. To understand the feelings which lie behind this placing against each other of two Arab concerns equally distasteful to Doughty—sexual love and Islam—is to begin to understand the nature of the emotional experience which is recorded in *Arabia Deserta*. We cannot fully agree with Lawrence, I think, that 'Doughty went among these people dispassionately, looked at their life, and wrote it down word for word', nor that 'by being always Arab in manner and European in mind he maintained a perfect judgment, while bearing towards them a full sympathy which persuaded them to show him their inmost ideas'.[17] At best, this is only what Doughty intended to do, and, fortunately, only partly accomplished.

Accurate factual reporting there is, of course. He saw no 'strewed skeletons of camels nor mounds of sand blown upon their fallen carcases' which had been reported concerning the trail left by the pilgrimage caravan, and he made it a point to correct the erroneous belief. Cattle are valuable to the Arabs and if an animal is about to die, they hastily slaughter it to make use of its meat and skin. And in the event that an animal must be abandoned, then the hyena, wolf, and carrion birds make short work of devouring it, and the bones must of necessity be scattered. Not only did Doughty never see 'any frame of bones lying in the desert or buried in the sand-driving wind', but he explains that the wind blows only lightly and seldom in inner Arabia (I, 96). He describes minutely the condition of the pilgrims, their poverty, and religious zeal, without offering very many clues to his own reactions. The Persians in the pilgrimage, for example, numbered 'near seven hundred'. They were 'girded in wadmel coats, falling below the knees, and thereunder wide cotton slops, upon their heads are furred caps as the Scandinavians'. These pilgrims 'lay up devoutly of their slender thrift for many years before, that they may once weary their lives in this great religious voyage' (I, 98). Always, he is aware of his surroundings—the fine sand under his feet, for example

(I, 97), 'in which for jollity, that we are come so far in the sacred way, the young Damascus serving men wallowed and flung one over other'.

He listened intently to the Arabs. He heard one explain that there were 'three kinds of Arabic utterance: *el-aly*, the lofty style as when a man should discourse with great personages: *el-wast*, the mean speech namely for the daily business of human lives; and that all broken, limping and thread-bare, *el-dûn*, the lowly—"and wellah as this speaking of Khalîl" '. Here he feels that he must defend himself and he explains to the reader that 'nevertheless that easy speech, which is born in the mouth of the Beduins, is far above all the school-taught language of the town'. (I, 168). He quickly learned the conventional terms of the nomads' speech. '*Eyyal amm* "brothers' children",' he explains, applies to all the members of a tribe. *Amm* primarily means paternal uncle, but he found that the Bedouins apply the term also to the host of a guest, to the 'father of a wife's child by her former husband', and to the master of a servant or slave. *Ibn akhy* means literally 'son of my brother', but the host uses the term in referring to his guest, and an older or more important person uses it in addressing one younger or less important. 'My father,' *abuy*, is the term of address used by the younger and lesser person in speaking to his superiors in age or position. 'Full of humanity is that gentle persuasion of theirs from their hearts,' he writes, 'for thy good, *ana abûk* "my word is faithful, I am thy father", or *ana akhûk*, "I am thy brother", *akhtak*, "thy sister", *umak*, "thy mother": and akin to these is a sublime work in Moses, which follows the divine commandments, "I am the Lord thy God" ' (I, 360–1).

Quite without overtones of personal reaction are some comments on Arab tribal life, its almost patriarchal form of government, moderate and humane. 'The nomad sheykhs,' he reports (I, 361–2), 'govern with a homely-wise moderation and providence; they are the peace-makers in the menzil (tribal meetings), and arbiters betwixt tribesmen.' But the tribesman's 'mind is ever in the Ghrazzu [raid]; the knave would win, and by whose loss he recks not, neither with what improbity; men in that squalid ignorance and extreme living, become wild'. Some, in spite of their straightened circumstances, 'are virtuous and higher human spirits' but 'human life, where the poor hardly find passage by foul and cragged ways, full of cruel gins, is spread out more evenly' for these, and they are the 'noblemen of the desert, men of ripe moderation, peacemakers of a certain erudite subtle judgment' (I, 301–2). Doughty leaves some ray of hope even for the Arab mentality. The Arabs, he thinks, have 'such facility of mind, that it seems they only lack the occasion, to speed in any way of learning'. But he feels he must qualify this judgment and he adds the unflattering limitation: 'that were by an easy imitation' (II, 56).

He explains that the 'soul in these Semites cleaveth to the dust', but their religious confidence 'is in a heaven nigh them, and the community of human kindness is largely round about them'. This is evidenced by the absence of suicide, 'the great offence of man's desolate spirit', among the Arabs. How can they despair of God's providence, he asks, when 'they see the Lord's hand working in all about them, the name of God is in their names, [and] they call upon God in every mouthful of words'. (I, 517). His experience with Arabic hospitality enabled him to explain its religious basis: every guest is a guest of God. But he very astutely observes that there may be another motive for the hospitality practised by the Arabs—the desire for the good opinion of their neighbours. Doughty does not labour this point; he puts it in the form of a 'saying' which he had heard 'in the mouths of town Arabians,—"It is for the report which passing strangers may say of them in the country: for the hosts beyond will be sure to ask of their guests, 'Where lodged ye the last night; and were ye well entertained' " ' (II, 259–60). But this observation touches upon a very important characteristic of Eastern peoples, their extremely high social consciousness; and in the desert the opinion of society was the only effective sanction of morality.

He also had opportunity to observe family life among the Arabs, and he writes that 'the woman's lot is here unequal concubinage, and in this necessitous life a weary servitude'. She passes from domination by her father to domination by her husband; she has no free choice in marriage, and may be put aside at the pleasure of her husband. Her only salvation is to bear many sons in order to ensure her place in the family unit. 'Few then are the nomad wives whose years can be long happy in marriage!' For 'what oneness of hearts can be betwixt these lemans, whose lots are not faithfully joined?' (I, 277–8). The lot of women in the towns is no easier; she is 'in bondage and her heart has little or no refreshment' (II, 376). By reproducing a conversation at the 'coffee' of Zeyd, his friendly host in the desert, he indicates clearly how deeply rooted was the custom of veiling the faces of married women. He argued against them that among the Arabs those tribes which were most strict in observing the custom were the most corrupted; but though he gained the acquiescence of Zeyd and those gathered about the coffee hearth, he could tell from the expression on their faces that they were thinking in their hearts, 'thou thinkest as the kuffâr [infidels]—the face of a wife should be seen of no man besides her own husband' (I, 280). The position of the husband in the family, he finds, is that of an absolute dictator. Even his intimate friend at Khebar, Mohammed Nejûmy, though he was amiable and gentle to his friends, 'was a soldier in his own house', ruling his wife and stepson with an iron hand (II, 160). But out in the desert, the children 'grow up without instruction of the parents'. They learn only from the proverbs and saws which they hear in the tents of the tribesmen and 'their only censor is the public opinion'. The father, he observes, was especially lenient with his son; and he explains that the poor Arab had only his son to comfort him in his old age and at last to bury him honourably and remember him. Thus the son was a man's link with the future, even that future which he would not live to see (I, 281–3).

Doughty is not always accurate in his judgments when he enlarges his observations with explanations. 'Rubba was a good simple man, though he never requited his hakîm [doctor, *i.e.*, Doughty] with a thank,' he complains (I, 475). The complaint betrays a lack of understanding of the Eastern belief that a poor man is entitled to the alms of the more fortunate. We have seen that Burton tried to explain the Easterner's attitude towards a benefactor, and Doughty himself seems to have some inkling of the attitude when he observes on another occasion (I, 384) that 'in the popular sort of nomads is little or no conscience to rob food (only); they holding it as common, kheyr Ullah [i.e., God's bounty]'. Again, he explains (I, 263) that attached to his host's family was 'an aged widow, in wretchedness, who played the mother to her dead daughter's fatherless children, a son so deformed that like a beast he crept upon the sand (*ya latif*, "oh happy sight!" said this most poor and desolate grandam, with religious irony, in her patient sighing)'. There may very well be religious irony in Doughty's interpretation of '*ya latif*', but it seems more probable that the old grandmother was calling upon her God, using one of the favourite Arabic names for the Deity ('Oh gracious One'). This would change the nature of the irony somewhat, and in the light of the meaning of Islam, make of the old woman something less of an oddity. In the bulk of the *Arabia Deserta* these are insignificant details. But it is well to keep in mind that Doughty was not perfectly attuned to the Arabic temper. He thought the Arabs 'men of little understanding', for example (I, 303), because they murmured 'It was an heathenish deed' when he unintentionally offended them by throwing on the fire some bushes which they considered the 'bread of the cattle' and which they would not destroy 'even in their enemies' country'. If the Arabs were 'of little understanding' for blaming him, certainly he was not understanding in refusing to accept gracefully the censure for what was to them so grievous an offence.

If *Arabia Deserta* had offered no more than such accurate reporting and fairly accurate exegesis, it would have been another interesting book about Arabia. It is a *great* book because upon the foundation of accurate detail Doughty has reproduced an emotional experience, a record of the struggle, both physical and psychical, between Khalîl and his traditions on the one hand and Arabia and the Arabs on the other.

4

Burton's strictures upon Doughty's knowledge of the Arabs are no more extreme than is his intimation that Doughty suffered only indignities and rebuffs at the hands of the Arabs. Miss Treneer (p. 39) rightly regrets that too little has been made of the 'friendlier, gentler side' of *Arabia Deserta*. She points out that Doughty had much satisfaction in the nomad life he led with the Fukura and Moahib Arabs. But he experienced some satisfaction and made friends among the town Arabs as well. 'He was very patient, generous and pitiful,' writes Lawrence, 'to be accepted into their confidence without doubt.' [18] And while there are many instances in *Arabia Deserta* which show clearly that the Arabs, both of the desert and of the towns, had many doubts about Khalîl, it is also true that Doughty was at times 'patient, generous, and pitiful'. There is in him a very deep and warm sense of the brotherhood of man, of the bond that holds humanity together. At Medáin Sâlih, for example, he notes that 'the well lining of rude stone courses, without mortar, is deeply scored, (who may look upon the like without emotion?) by the soft cords of many nomad generations' (I, 145). He coupled this sympathy with 'an unflattering plainness of speech' which he thought was 'agreeable to the part of sûwahh, or wandering anchorite in the fable of human life' and 'by gentleness and good faith' he felt that he was able to win over the Arabs, even those who were initially violent foes (II, 59).

At El-Ally (I, 191) when the children jeeringly cried after him 'Aha! the Nasrâny [Nazarene, or Christian]' the elder men 'turned to rebuke them', and when he sat among them in their gatherings they often preached the 'comfortable text', '*kul wahed aly din-hu*, "every one in his own religion" '. At Hâyil (II, 62–3) when he came to his host's 'coffee' the young son baited him with 'Ho! Nasrâny, thou canst not look to the heaven!' Doughty gently answered, 'See, my son, I may look upon it as well . . . as another and better;—*taal húbbiny*! come thou and kiss me.' And he won over many a young courtier of Ibn Rashîd when he answered the taunt '*Fen rubbuk*, "Where is thy Lord God?" ' with '*Fi kull makán*, "The Lord is in every place"; which word of the Nasrâny pleased them strangely, and was soon upon all their tongues in the Kasr [castle].' Even at Kheybar where he suffered ignominiously (II, 160–1), he was able to make at least one sincere friend, Mohammed, whom he affectionately and respectfully called *Amm*. Mohammed's wife was a nomad, a Beduwîa, with whom Doughty was very sympathetic. He describes an occasion when Mohammed rose to strike his son: 'The Beduwîa ran between them to shelter her stepson, though to her the lad was not kind. I caught the Nejûmy's arm, yet his force bruised the poor woman;—and, "wellah, she said, smiling in her tears to see the tempest abated, thy hand Mohammed is heavy, and I think has broken some of my bones".' When he left Kheybar he tried to repay his host with some medicines, a new tunic, and a new gun-stock.

Mohammed was displeased: 'Nay, Khalîl, but leave me happy with the remembrance, and take it not away from me by requiting me! only this I desire of thee that thou sometimes say, "*The Lord remember him for good.*" ' Doughty persuaded him to receive the gifts, but felt that he had sinned in so doing, against that 'charitable integrity, the human affection, which was in Amm Mohammed; and which, like the waxen powder upon summer fruits, is deflowered under any rude handling'. 'When he received my gift,' he explains, 'it seemed to him that I had taken away his good works!' (II, 233). Often the townspeople urged Doughty to profess Islam and to settle among them. They offered him their women that he might choose a wife. At Hâyil his friends talked about the 'Jew-born Abdullah' who was happy in his new religion and who refused to receive the offers of his parents to welcome him back among them. 'He had forsaken the Law and the Promises,' writes Doughty, 'but a man who is moved by the affections of human nature, may not so lightly pass from all that in which he has been cherished and bred up in the world!' (I, 154–5).

He received offers of marriage from the Bedouins as well. Zeyd, one of the sheikhs with whom he lived in the desert, offered him one of his two wives (I, 365). He found Zeyd's Arabs friendly. 'The few good women,' he writes (I, 367), 'sorted with worthy men, to whom they have borne sons, are seen of comely, and hardly less than matronly carriage' and they all came to him to examine his medicines. He was happy to leave the towns and oasis settlements for these were full of religious fanatics; he preferred to cast his lot with the Bedouins and for a very little money which would enable the needy nomads to buy 'a shirt-cloth and mantle' he was able to make journeys 'among lawless and fanatical tribes' in safety (I, 614). The nomads were never brutal, he found (I, 384), and often they were considerate and kind. When he was weak from hunger and stood gazing at the equally hungry Arabs as they sweated over their task of drawing water for their camels (I, 507), he appealed to their generosity in the name of God to draw for his camel also. 'God help, thee, Khalîl,' they said, 'and have no care for this, but sit down, that it is we will water her.' After the terrible ordeal of fasting through Ramadan, the Bedouins made holiday and insisted that Khalîl show them the

English holiday dance. He was afraid that his refusal would 'make a breach in their mirth', but because he could foresee their unsophisticated judgment, he was 'half-ashamed to show them the manner'. The simple Arabs were amazed: ' "Oh! what was that outlandish skipping and casting of the shanks, and this footing it to and fro!"—it seemed to them a morris dance! but when they heard more, of our carolling, that his arm about her middle, every man danced it forth bosom to bosom with every fair woman, they thought of us but scorn and villany [sic]' (I, 607). Sometimes they asked him of Christian fasting and when he told them of the lenient custom of fast among the Christians they were incredulous: ' "Ah-ha-ha! but you call this fast? nay wellah, Khalîl, you laugh and jest!"— "But they think it a fasting diet, 'as the death', in those plentiful countries,—to eat such weak wretchedness and poor man's victuals."—"God is Almighty! Well, that were a good fasting!—and they cried between wonder and laughter—Oh that the Lord would give us thus every day to fast!" ' (I, 588).

During the month of fasting Doughty watched Zeyd's sister keeping her Lent, 'neither eating nor drinking until the long going-down of the sun', while she 'suckled her babe'. He was full of pity and admiration for the 'good woman, and kind mother, a strenuous housewife, full of affectionate service and sufferance to the poor man her husband' (I, 586). In the season of famine he also derived spiritual pleasure from lying under the clear heavens and contemplating the brilliant stars. He mused:

> In a land of enemies, I have found more refreshment than upon beds and pillows in our close chambers.—Hither lies no way from the city of the world, a thousand years pass as one daylight; we are in the world and not in the world, where Nature brought forth man, an enigma to himself, and an evil spirit sowed in him the seeds of dissolution. And, looking then upon that infinite spectacle, this life of the wasted flesh seemed to me ebbing, and the spirit to waver her eyas wings unto that divine obscurity (I, 520).

In the desert the periods of hunger and privation sharpened his senses and his sensibility. It became a pleasure to listen to the 'cheerful musing Beduin talk, a lesson in the traveller's school of mere humanity, he may not pass, for man is of one mind everywhere, ay, and in their kind, even the brute animals of the same foster earth'. Even 'the sounds of the spretting milk under the udders in the Arabs' vessels' gladdened him (I, 305).

There were times when he became magnanimous. He patiently taught a sheikh's wife the lesson of 'wifely meekness' which accomplished the end which she had hoped to attain by asking Khalîl to write for her an *hijâb*, or charm, which would prevent her husband from divorcing her (I, 512). He explained to the indigent Arabs that their almsgiving was not in vain, impressing them with the Scriptural text, 'He who giveth alms lendeth to the Lord: and as you sow so shall you reap hereafter.' He talked to them about an after life and tried to banish their fears of Îblis and Sheytân, childish fears of Satan. They did not understand his 'marvellously quaint' lore, but he did not rail at them, or condemn them for their ignorance, for he was touched by the motives of their questions: they were anxious to know if they would meet again their fathers and friends who had gone before them (I, 493–4). His sense of the warm humanity of mankind was strengthened by the poor nomads who ran out to milk a camel for him, a 'wayfaring man, even though the poor owners should go supperless themselves (I, 256)' and by the very honourable sheikh Thaifullah (Guest of God) who would not take even a little tobacco from the stranger whom he was entertaining. 'These were simple, pious and not (formal) praying Arabs, having in their mouths no cavilling questions of religion, but they were of the godly humanity of the wilderness' (II, 83).

5

But the warmer, friendlier side of *Arabia Deserta* is but a part of the whole. Physical discomfort, constant fear of death, and racial and religious prejudice frequently overshadow the basic humanity of Khalîl and produce the many climaxes in *Arabia Deserta* by bringing into prominence the enmity between the Arabs and their guest. Miss Treneer (p. 40) believes that we must not 'be too much inclined to take him at his word' when we read that 'he had but one good day in Arabia; that all the others were made bitter to him by the fanaticism of his hosts';

Doughty 'was always apt to speak out of the vexation of the moment', she explains. But it is this vexation which animates the major portion of *Arabia Deserta*. 'It is a passion to be a pointing-stock for every finger and to maintain even a just opinion against the half-reason of the world,' Doughty writes (II, 68), and 'I have felt this in the passage of Arabia more than the daily hazards and long bodily sufferance'. And there was always a good climate for his vexation, for, as Fairley observes, 'for all his sympathetic understanding of them [the Arabs], he is never intimate with them, nor they with him. In almost every case the breach is more powerful than the bond, and for the most part he is among enemies. Even behind their friendliness there usually lurks a threat.' [19]

The source of all his suffering in Arabia, according to Doughty, was the 'Turkishness' of the British Consul at Damascus who would not give him official protection of the British Government. Even an 'informal benevolent word', thought Doughty, would have procured for him the 'regard of the great Haj officers, and their letters of commendation, in departing from them, to the Emirs of Arabia'. Out of his vexation he wrote (I, 40): 'There is a merry saying of Sir Henry Wotton, for which he nearly lost his credit with his sovereign, "An ambassador is a man who is sent to lie abroad for his country"; to this might be added, "A Consul is a man who is sent to play the Turk abroad, to his own countrymen." '

It is no wonder that he immediately began to experience difficulty in this land where 'the name of Nasrâny was yet an execration', and where 'even among the nomads a man will say to another, "Dost thou take me for a Nasrâny! that I should do such (iniquitous) thing" ' (I, 635). The camel-master of the Persian group with which Doughty was travelling in the first stages of the great pilgrimage sometimes refused to send him his camel when the signal shot was fired; 'when it happened thus, I laid hold of el-Eswad, and would not let him go, for though they brought up the beast at last, I had not the strength to load on her single handed: sometimes the worst have sworn to "leave my body under the sand where I stood" '. When the danger was urgent, he writes, 'I drew out before them my naked pistol: after other days, they gave over thus to trouble me. They are wolves to each other and what if some were hounds to me? For the distress of the way edges all men's spirits' (I, 107). Whey they had reached Medáin Sâlih where he was to leave the caravan, Doughty was again in difficulty. The Persian whom he had hired to conduct him on the pilgrimage now refused to transport his baggage 'because his covenant was out'. Doughty had given him medicines on the way and now he mused, 'These gracious Orientals are always graceless short-comers at the last, and therefore may they never thrive!' (I, 125). His generalizations extended even to the 'Persian lordlings for whom was pitched a wide pavilion in the stations' of the pilgrimage: 'but for that little I met with them, I could imagine the solemn Persian gentlemen to be the most bad hearted dunghill souls of all nations'. His own Persian hosts 'came little behind them in the Persian birth of their minds, save that leading their lives in Damascus, they were pleasant smilers as the Arabs' (I, 100).

Despite the great danger of doing so, burning resentment often drove him to speak out boldly. When the Arabs taunted him with the Christian habit of eating 'swine's flesh' he retaliated with a long list of Arab food not generally considered 'clean': 'I see you eat crows and kites, and the lesser carrion eagle. Some of you eat owls, some eat serpents, the great lizard you all eat, and locusts, and the spring-rat; many eat the hedgehog, in certain (Hejâz) villages they eat rats, you cannot deny it! you eat the wolf too, and the fox and the foul hyena, in a word, there is nothing so vile that some of you will not eat' (I, 584). To show his resentment he refused to make room for Sheykh Sâlih at a coffee gathering. He said sullenly,' Sâlih . . . may find another seat.' And when one of the group murmured at this lack of respect, Doughty 'turned and said to him plainly, "I have wandered in many lands, many years, and with a swine such as thou art, I have not met in any place."' He reports that 'the timid Hejâz audience were astonished at my words' (II, 135). During the season of famine in the desert, he went to the tent of Darŷesh, 'the Serahîny sheykh, a very fond and scolding splenetic person', to beg of him a bowl of milk. Darŷesh was not in a giving mood and he had no love for Khalîl: 'This dog-face,' writes Doughty, 'whom I had often seen in Tollog's kahwa [coffee] tent, always professed against me a fanatical bitter enmity; he shot through me with his glancing eyes at the mejlis, but had never spoken with the kafir [infidel]!' Certainly the mere asking of milk of such an enemy was indiscreet. 'If I might find thee one day in the wilderness,' threatened the sheikh, 'and my gun were in my hand, then would I shoot thee dead!' Doughty spoke up boldly and challenged him to shoot, promising that his own shot would not spare the Arab. 'Take thy gun to-morrow, except thou be'st a coward, and fire thy shot, and I will fire another; by the Lord I think not to spare thee.' His boldness won for him the friendship of those sitting with Darŷesh, and so he gained his bowl of milk (I, 508).

But such tactics achieved only initial successes, for he did not have the physical strength with which to support this attitude. Nor could he hope to overcome with a few bold words an hereditary hatred of Christians. When he walked for relaxation along the outskirts of a settlement, the children, without the older men to rebuke them, flocked about him with swords and bats 'hooting, "O Nasrâny! O Nasrâny!"' and they chanted vile carols accompanied with appropriate gestures (I, 198). His boldness sometimes resulted in physical punishment; he had his beard plucked, was slapped and spit upon (I, 305-7). And many a fanatical townsman promised him immediate death, 'except thou say the testimony' (II, 424).

Often he was able to avert disaster by showing his helplessness. Struggling on foot to keep up with two soldiers who were urging their mules to a faster pace for fear of being overtaken and attacked by raiding Bedouins, he desperately clung to the saddles to help himself along, until one of the soldiers, seeing he could go no further, bade the other dismount. They helped him to the saddle although all three knew well enough that it would have been easier to abandon Khalîl, and with impunity (I, 179). On other occasions he threw himself upon the mercy of some Arab by uttering '*dakhîl-ak*', the formula which commands the protection of an Arab because it appeals to his sense of religious duty.

Thus he was saved from abandonment in the wilderness by appealing to Kasîm (II, 79–80), and saved from possible death at the hands of slaves at Khebar by appealing to the mercy of Imbârak (II, 72). But these, too, were temporary reliefs and he suffered 'distress of soul, to kick against the fanaticism of the whole Ishmaelite country' (I, 501). He offered his torments at

Khebar as a warning to those who would come there either to convert the Arabs or to investigate the town's ancient Hebrew origin: 'I would that these leaves might save the deaths of some: and God give me this reward for my labour! for who will, he may read in them all the tale of Khebar' (II, 146).

Certainly Doughty's religious sentiments influenced the emotional experience recorded in *Arabia Deserta*. Burton concluded that one lesson suggested by the book is 'the need for a certain pliancy in opinion, religious and political' in a traveller:[20] and Achmed Abdullah felt that Doughty's 'particular brand of medieval, narrow, intolerant Protestant Christianity' prevented him from getting to the 'roots of an alien faith and civilization'.[21] Sympathetic critics, too, have noted the importance of Doughty's religious position: R. Ellis Roberts was sure that Doughty's relations with the Arabs were 'direct, sincere, instinctive, just because his point of view is remote and separate';[22] and Anne Treneer (p. 46) observed that 'most of [Doughty's] troubles came because he proclaimed himself a Christian'. It would be difficult and perhaps not necessary to decide upon the formal name of Doughty's religion.[23] But it *is* important to note his interest in the Bible. The book is full of Biblical allusions: the long street in Damascus was 'that which in Paul's days was called "The Straight" '; the ruined city called *Umm Jemmâl* was 'in Jeremiah Beth Gamul'; and the watering place named *Zerka* was 'the Biblical Jabbok, a border of the children of Amman in Moses' days' (I, 42-51).

The interest is not, I think, narrowly religious. In the preface to the second edition of *Arabia Deserta* he explains, as we have seen, that his decision to penetrate Arabia was born of the desire to investigate inscriptions which were reportedly to be found at Medáin Sâlih. All that was known of these inscriptions was that they were not Arabic, and because he was interested 'in all that pertains to Biblical research', he resolved to 'accept the hazard of visiting them' (I, 31). A further clue to the nature of his interest he gives in the preface to the third edition, in which he likened the life of the nomad Arabs to that 'which was followed by their ancestors, in the Biblical tents of Kedar'. He wrote that the speech and customs of the Arabs carry us 'back to the days of the nomad Hebrew Patriarchs', and that by becoming familiar with present day nomadic life 'we are the better able to read the bulk of the Old Testament books, with that further insight and understanding, which comes of a living experience'.

Thus he is constantly musing on the humanity of the ancients. The towers and hewed cisterns along the way of the pilgrimage route remind him that 'the tower was always the hope of this insecure Semitic world, so that Jehovah is lauded as "a Tower of Salvation, a strong tower from the enemy, a strong tower in His name"' (I, 52). Observing that there were no watches or clocks in the Arab villages, but that they 'take their wit in the day-time, by the shadowing-round of a little wand set upon the channel brink', he thought of the 'dial of which we read in Job: "a servant earnestly desireth the shadow ... our days on the earth are a shadow"' (II, 220). And when he found chipped flints in a dry river bed at Maan, he wondered at 'that old human kindred' which must have dwelt in the land before its occupation by the Semitic race: 'Does not the word of Isaiah, there imitating perhaps the people's *argot*, come to our hearts concerning them?—"What was the rock whence ye were hewn, and the hole of the pit whence ye were digged"' (I, 74).

It is the humanity of Christianity that he sets up against the religion of Mohammed. 'And what seek we in religion?' he asks, '—is it not the perfect law of humanity?—to bind up the wounds, and heal the sores of human life; and a pathway to heaven.' So he wondered at the 'diversity of the Semitic faiths': 'the Messianic religion—a chastisement of the soul sunning herself in the divine love—were fain to cast her arms about the human world, sealing all men one brotherhood with a virginal kiss of meekness and charity'; but 'the Mohammedan chain-of-credulities is an elation of the soul, breathing of God's favour only to the Moslemîn: and shrewdness out of her cankered bowels to all the world besides' (II, 406–7).

We have seen that he grudgingly admired Islam because the great faith in Divine Providence among its adherents made suicide a rarity. But suicide, he believed, was madness which should be prevented by humanity:

> In the ferment of our civil societies, from which the guardian angels seem to depart, we see many every moment sliding at

the brink. What anguishes are rankling in the lees of the soul, the heart-nipping unkindness of a man's friends, his defeated endeavours! betwixt the birth and death of the mind, what swallowing seas, and storms of mortal miseries! And when the wildfire is in the heart and he is made mad, the incontinent hands would wreak the harm upon his own head, to blot out the abhorred illusion of the world and the desolate remembrance of himself. Succoured in the forsaken hour, when his courage swerved, with the perfume of human kindness, he might have been to-day alive. Many have looked for consolation, in the imbecility of their souls, who found perhaps hardness of face and contradiction; they perished untimely in default of our humanity (I, 517).

The significance of this passage, coming as it does so hard upon his admiration of the lack of suicides among the Moslems, is more readily seen in Doughty's remarks on asceticism, which occur in the same section of the book. He makes it perfectly clear that asceticism is an evil means to a good end:

And I mused in these nights and days of the old hermits of Christian faith that were in the upper desert countries—and there will rise up some of the primitive temper in every age to renew and judge the earth; how there fled many wilfully from the troublesome waves of the world, devising in themselves to retrieve the first Adam in their own souls, and coveting a sinless habitation with the elements, whither, saving themselves out of the common calamities, they might accomplish the time remaining of their patience, and depart to better life. A natural philosophy meditates the goodly cure; religious asceticism is sharp surgery to cut away the very substance of man's faulty affections; sorting wonderfully with that fantastic pride and maidish melancholy which is also of the human soul, that has weariness of herself in the world, and some stains even in the shortest course. The soul that would rid herself out of all perplexed ways, desireth in her anger even the undoing of this hostile body, only ground of her disease.

The very next sentence reveals Doughty's way of pitting against each other things with which he is unsympathetic. Previously we noted his use in this way of 'Aphrodisiastic modulations' and the 'New austerity of a masculine religion'; in this instance it is religious fanaticism and religious asceticism: 'Mohammed bade spare that pale generation of walkers-apart, men of prayer blackened in the desert, a kind of spiritual Nimrods, going about in fairy-land of religion to build of themselves a stair to heaven.' The two-front attack is continued in the next sentence, emphasis now being placed on Mohammed's ulterior motive and the ascetics' folly: 'And cause was that certain of them, "having the spirit of prophecy", had saluted in the young caravaner the secret signs of his further apostleship.' And finally the argument is concluded:

> But Mohammed in the koran, with the easy felicity of the Arabian understanding, notes the heartless masking of these undoers, for God, of themselves and the human brotherhood: 'Ullah sent the Evangil by his apostle Îsa-bin-miriam, unto the Christian nation; but the way of the Eremites is out of their own finding' (I, 520–1).

But Doughty's lack of sympathy with Mohammed and his religion is revealed not only in such subtleties as 'bade spare', 'cause was', and 'easy felicity of the Arabian understanding'. He records the fact that treasurers of the pilgrimage were Christians and that 'we always find aliens taken to these trusts, in the Mohammedan governments'. The reason for this is clear; for, 'Mohammed has made every follower of his, with his many spending and vanishing wives, a walker upon quicksands; but Christ's religion contains a man in all, which binds him in single marriage' (I, 63). He found in the circumstances of the arduous pilgrimage evidence of the inhumanity of Islam because of 'that yearly suffering and sacrifice of human flesh, and all lost labour, for a vain opinion, a little salt of science would dissolve all their religion!' (I, 92). One of the Persians who spent a large portion of each year in the service of the pilgrimage was 'a pined and jaded man . . . before his middle days, and unlikely to live to full age. Better his mother had been barren, than that her womb should have borne such a sorry travailous life' (I, 99). There is no doubt, I think, that at the bottom of all his philosophic criticism of Islam is his love for humanity. 'Religion,' he writes, 'when she possesses the better minds is amiable, humane, and liberal; but corrupting in envious disgraced natures must needs give up some baneful breath of self-loving and fanaticism, which passes among them for laudable fruit of the spirit that is of their religious patriotism.' Religion itself, and patriotism are noble: 'In the one and the other there seem to us to be sweetly comprehended all virtues; and yet in the excess they are springs from which flow out extreme mischiefs.'[24] It is the excess of these in Islam which made him cry out that 'The Arabian religion of the sword must be tempered by the sword: and were the daughter of Mecca and Medina led captive, the Moslemîn should become as Jews' (II, 406). It is ironic that his feeling for humanity should suggest such inhuman measures.

6

In his introduction to *Arabia Deserta* Lawrence observed that there were two kinds of Englishmen abroad. One group, he thought, tried to adjust themselves to foreign surroundings, tried to imitate the natives, but 'they cannot avoid the consequences of the imitation, a hollow worthless thing'. The other class was the larger; 'in the same circumstance of exile they reinforce their character by memories of the life they have left . . . they take refuge in the England that was theirs . . . they assert aloofness, their immunity, the more vividly for their loneliness and weakness'. And what is more important, 'they impress the peoples among whom they live by reaction, by giving them an ensample of the complete Englishman, the foreigner intact'. 'Doughty,' he concluded, 'is a member of the second, the cleaner class.' Lawrence was a frequent visitor of both Doughty and Blunt, and it is impossible not to assume that Blunt is to be placed in the first class. Certainly, according to these premises Doughty is 'the complete Englishman'. His patriotism, at times approaching jingoism, is most obvious in his poetry and especially in *The Cliffs* and *The Clouds*. But even in the *Arabia Deserta* there is sufficient evidence that his patriotism and pride of race influenced the nature of the relationship between the traveller and the Arabs. They could not understand, for example, that the 'Engleys have a Queen, and no man to rule over them!' and Doughty answered by translating the Queen's name into '*Mansur, The Victorious Lady*: a name which (used in the masculine) is also of happy augury in their tongue' (II, 402). Doughty does not explain that the word *mansur* may have had the connotation of 'conqueror', and 'conqueror by God's help' to the Arabs. The Arabs were also perplexed by the Englishman's account of the number of fighting men which his nation could put in the field, and he calmed their fears by assuring them that 'we, being the stronger, make no unjust wars: ours is a religion of peace; the weak may live in quietness for us', and he proudly explained that England 'had made the great war of *Krîm* (the Crimea) for the Sultan and their sake' (I, 318). At 'Ayn ez-Zeyma, thirty miles from the coast and last station before Mecca along the pilgrimage route, Moslem hatred of the Christian was extreme. There Doughty bolstered the prestige of England while he passed the time, 'disarmed their insolence, and damped the murderous mind in Sâlem' (who had threatened him with death), by calling the Arab's attention to some loads of Indian rice stacked before the public meeting place. 'What sacks be these?' he asked them, 'and the letters of them? if any of you (ignorant persons) could read letters? Shall I tell you?' And the naïve semi-nomads of the tiny hamlet who knew nothing of world trade and British Imperialism listened incredulously to the hated Christian's explanation that 'this is the rice of the Engleys, in sacks of the Engleys; and the marks are words of the Engleys'. 'You go well clad!' he continued, 'though only hareem wear this blue colour in the north! but what tunics are these?—I tell you, the cotton on your backs was spun and wove in mills of the Engleys. Ye have not considered that ye are fed in part and clothed by the Engleys!' (II, 525–6).

At times Doughty steps out of the character of Khalîl and speaks directly to his countrymen. The following is an account of his questioning of a slave at Khebar.

'Of what nation were the slave drivers?'—this he could not answer: they were white men, and in his opinion Moslemîn; but not Arabians, since they were not at home at *Jidda*, which was then, *and is now the staple town of African slavery, for the Turkish Empire:—Jidda where are Frankish consuls!* But you shall find these worthies, in the pallid solitude of their palaces, affecting (great Heaven!) the simplicity of new-born babes, —they will tell you, they are not aware of it! But I say again, in your ingenuous ears, *Jidda is the staple town of the Turkish slavery*, OR ALL MOSLEMÎN ARE LIARS (II, 187).

Having heard a rumour that a Christian had been slain the year before at Mecca, he indignantly declares that the Christian nations have suffered such 'religious brigandage' too long. 'Why have they no Residents,' he asks, 'for the police of nations in Mecca?' And 'why have they not occupied the direful city in the name of the health of nations, in the name of the common religion of humanity, *and because the head of the slave trade is there?*' And he suggests that 'it were good for the Christian governments, which hold any of the Mohammedan provinces, to consider that till then they may never quietly possess them', for 'each year at Mecca every other name is trodden down, and the "Country of the Apostle" is they pretend inviolable, where no worldly power may reach them. It is "The City of God's house",—and the only God is God only of the Moslemîn' (II, 68). In another passage he interrupts his report of a conversation between the pilgrimage officers concerning him —a conversation containing threats to the Nasrâny if he should dare to follow the pilgrimage beyond Medáin Sâlih—to address his readers: 'Englishmen, who help these barbarians at Constantinople that cannot be taught, they would murder you secretly, and let hounds live, at Medina and Mecca!' (I, 248).

It is impossible in *Arabia Deserta*, I think, to separate Doughty's strong racial and national instincts from his humanitarianism. It may be possible to do so in his poetry, as Barker Fairley suggests,[25] but in his prose there are but few passages which might perhaps be attributable to his national and racial instincts alone. For example, noting the Arab townspeople's corrupt speech, he digresses to pass judgment on Victorian English and to indicate distress at its lack of dignity: 'The strong contagion of a false currency in speech we must needs acknowledge with "harms at the heart" in some land where we are not strangers!—where after Titanic births of the mind there remains to us an illiberal remissness of language which is not known in any barbarous nation.'[26] This is not merely an idle comment, for language was a serious matter with Doughty and indeed he indicated in a letter to Hogarth that one of the reasons for writing the *Arabia Deserta* was the desire to improve Victorian prose.[27] And the style of the book, of course, is the result of a conscious attempt to make the English language more indicative of national traditions. At another point in *Arabia Deserta* he explains that he took infinite pains to examine the Arabs that he might glean from them every possible bit of information which would help the cause of European study of geography (I, 469). And the book is full of geographical information and accompanied by a detailed map of Northwestern Arabia. Finally, perhaps his hope (I, 295) that any who come after him in Arabia will find the '(before reproachful) Christian name respectable over large provinces of the fanatical Peninsula', is prompted by racial rather than religious instincts, for in the 'seventies the Arabs of the area considered 'Christian' and 'English' synonymous.

But usually these instincts or prejudices are inextricably bound together; the instincts merge to become a pride in the faith that England is the greatest civilizing force in the world. The feeling, I think, animates Doughty's arguments with the Arabs and it is especially evident in his pronouncements on slavery. At 'Ayn ez-Zeyma, for example, he was overheard assuring African slaves that if the English had met with the traders who held them captive they would have set the slaves free and given them a home on English controlled territory. One of those who had overheard him gave him the lie and Doughty answered with the boast: 'By this you may know if I lie:—when I come to Jidda, bring a bondman to my Konsulato: and let the bondservant say he would be free, and he shall be free indeed!' In the Arab's answer Doughty underscores an appeal to his countrymen: 'Dog! cries the fellow, thou liar!—*are there not thousands of slaves at Jidda, that every day are bought and sold*? wherefore, thou dog! be they not all made free? if thou sayest sooth' (II, 524).

Without the proper conditioning of an understanding of the pain, hunger, weariness, scorn, and danger which Doughty experienced, and without a sympathy for the religious and racial bent of his mind, readers must attribute Doughty's contempt for the Arabs either to the blindness of bigotry or to the darkness of ignorance. But he is neither bigoted nor ignorant. I think his rantings are rather the manifestations of a thwarted inclination to sympathize with the Arabs, the inclination to see in them the strains of his own deep-rooted feelings of the brotherhood of mankind. Barker Fairley, even without the information that Doughty had the idea of *The Dawn in Britain* in his mind from the age of twenty-five, traced Doughty's wanderings and concluded that whether he realized it or not Doughty was attempting to work back to the origins of mankind. The motivation of the search, he thinks, was Doughty's deep love of England and its origins, the theme of *The Dawn in Britain*.[28] The combination of physical circumstances and temperamental incompatibility with the kind of religious-racial spirit which he found in Arabia produced the tension in *Arabia Deserta*. In this light, the rantings against the Arabs and their religion take on the deeper significance of Doughty's bitterness and disappointment. Expressions such as 'dreadful-faced harpy of their religion', 'sour Waháby fanaticism', and 'their souls are canker-weed beds of fanaticisms' (I, 95) are a far cry from the techniques of factual reporting.

In praising the appropriateness of Doughty's archaic style in the *Arabia Deserta*, Barker Fairley (pp. 22-30) notes three levels of irony in the book: the ironies of the Arabic speech which Doughty reproduced, Khalîl's ironic comments to the Arabs, and the irony of Doughty's detachment from Khalîl. Perhaps the disappointments revealed in Doughty's contempt for the Arabs, usually addressed to the reader and not always in archaic style, constitute another level. He explains to the reader (I, 253) that his Arab friends tried to persuade him to accept Islam outwardly that he might have safe passage in Arabia, and to believe inwardly whatever he would. He admits that these were 'words not far from wisdom' but though 'it had cost me little or naught, to confess Konfuchu or Socrates to be apostles of Ullah: ... I could not find it in my life to confess the barbaric prophet of Mecca and enter, under the yoke, into their solemn fools' paradise'. 'The Mohammedan theology,' he writes, 'is ineptitude so evident that it were only true in the moon.' During the Moslem Ramadan he found it difficult to 'altogether escape (that contagious pestilence of minds) the Mohammedan zelotism' which 'in these countries harbours in the more depravedly embodied of human souls' (I, 599).

In a passage which begins as a factual recording of the

diseases which most afflict the Arabs, Doughty suddenly inserts 'the ignominy of the Meccawy's religion' to describe the complaint of 'inability' (II, 18). The Moslem's ceremonial purifications he calls 'certain loathsome washings' (I, 99), and 'the holy hajjàj [pilgrims]' are a 'motley army, spotted guile is in their Asiatic hearts more than religion' (I, 101). And he ridicules the Moslem law which demands that prayers be said in Arabic: 'The litany of Mohammed's Arabian religion must be said in his native tongue—Oh what contempt in religions of the human reason! But it is a wonder to hear these poor foreigners [Persians], how they mouthe it, to say their prayer in the canonical strange speech, and only their clerkish men can tell what!' (I, 108.) Without having been to Mecca, and never himself having believed in Islam, he is yet able to inform the reader that when the pilgrims get to Mecca and look into the ark 'they see but bubbles burst, that seemed before pearls in Syria!' (I, 107). And what many travellers thought was very solemn and touching, 'the muethin crying from the minaret to the latter prayer', Doughty calls 'the abhorred voice of their barbaric religion!' (II, 341).

Doughty is fairly lenient in his criticism of Mohammed as a man, but he has nothing but contempt for him as the founder of Islam. 'The most venerable image in their minds,' he says of the Arabs, 'is the personage of Mohammed; which to us is less tolerable.' He admits Mohammed's 'mildness and comity and simplicity and good faith, in things indifferent of the daily life', but these, he thinks, 'cannot amend our opinion of the Arabian man's barbaric ignorance, his sleight and murderous cruelty in the institution of his religious faction; or sweeten our contempt of an hysterical prophetism and polygamous living' (II, 405). Of Islam he says, 'The old Semitic currencies in religion were uttered new under that bastard stamp of the (expedite, factious, and liberal) Arabian spirit, and digested to an easy sober rule of human life, (a pleasant carnal congruity looking not above men's possibility).' He is disturbed that 'Mohammed's saws' are the basis of the faith of a tenth of humanity. 'What had the world been?' he asks, 'if the tongue had not wagged, of this fatal Ishmaelite!' And while he has no fear of 'a thin-witted religion' in itself, yet he is apprehensive of any 'bond which can unite many of the human millions, for living and dying!' He couples

Islam and 'the commonwealth of Jews' as 'great secret conspiracies, friends only of themselves and to all without of crude iniquitous heart, unfaithful, implacable', and he is sure that 'the nations of Islam, of a barbarous fox-like understanding, and persuaded in their religion, that "knowledge is only of the koran", cannot now come upon any way that is good' (I, 141-2). And 'their religion', he warns, 'is murderous, and were therefore to be trodden out as fire by the humanity of the world' (I, 124).

There is yet another level of irony in *Arabia Deserta*, I think—one which may discomfort the sensitive modern reader. Doughty was not a wealthy man as was Blunt, nor did he travel under the auspices of governments and societies as did Burton. Uninvited and unwanted, Doughty entered Arabia with a few pieces of gold and a small package of medicines. For two years he depended for the most part on the hospitality of the Arabs. Certainly, then, he is speaking from the depths of weariness and disappointment when he says (II, 243) that 'the ill-faith of the Arabs is a gulf to cast in the teeth of the unwary! there is nothing to hope for in man, amongst them'. And it is perhaps more indicative of Doughty's state of mind than of the Arabs' mentality when he describes a nomad tribe as having a 'rat-like understanding' (I, 325). He writes that the Arabs in their group prayers were 'bowing the empty foreheads and falling upon the petticoated knees together' (I, 558), and that 'in their greediness to spoil the castaway life, whom they will not help forward, the Arabs are viler than any nation' (I, 621). And finally, he explains that an Arab, 'to clear himself of an unjust suspicion . . . will say to the other, "There is nothing between us but Ullah." Like words we hear from gentle Jonathan's mouth, in his covenant with the climbing friend David' (I, 310).

'The haps that befel me are narrated in these volumes:' he writes in the preface to the second edition, 'wherein I have set down, that which I saw with my eyes, and heard with my ears and thought in my heart, neither more nor less.' Nothing could better describe the realism of *Arabia Deserta*. The book is a detailed journal without the divisions according to dates, and its appropriateness is remarkable. It begins with belated preparations, after disappointments at the hands of the British Consul, for joining the pilgrimage which had already removed to the first station on its march. The sense of rushing, disorganization, the feeling of being at the mercy of those who are unsympathetic, and the fear of danger—all these characteristics of the plight of Khalîl in the book as a whole—are touched in this beginning. Throughout the two-year journey one climax follows upon another, each of which could easily have been the last ordeal of the traveller, until finally there occurs the happy sight of Jidda on the coast and the end of danger. With a masterstroke of restraint Doughty writes in a final, one-sentence paragraph: 'On the morrow I was called to the open hospitality of the British Consulate.' The natural chronology of the events forms an artistic organization and Doughty's artistry is evident in his refusal to violate the chronology. As Barker Fairley has observed (p. 94), when Doughty had to depend on his imagination for organization in *The Dawn in Britain* he chose a form resembling that which was dictated to him by historical circumstances in *Arabia Deserta*. The climaxes themselves—difficulties with 'rafîks' ('companions' or 'guides' with the added connotation of 'protector') who become faithless, danger of death at the hands of fanatical Moslems, and suffering from hunger and deprivation—have a recurring sameness which reinforces the physical monotony of the desert. We have already considered the effect of 'the haps that befel' him on what Doughty 'thought in [his] heart', and we have tried to suggest that his experiences in Arabia reacted upon his hopes and inclinations in such a way as to produce mingled feelings of satisfaction and disappointment.

What he 'saw with [his] eyes' related to his thoughts about the ancients and about the origins of the human family. We have seen that his decision to enter into Arabia was made when he heard about inscriptions at Medáin Sâlih. The following passage indicates the interest which the landscape of Arabia held for him:

> When we had ridden in the valley two hours, we came by many builded heaps, *rijûm*, in the midst of this wilderness of banks and stones. Certain of them I saw built up in part from a torrent channel;—had the seyl [stream] beds ceased to be ways of water in those old builders' days? Are those the graves of their sheykhly families?—but of what antiquity?

The upland Semitic life is ever rude, thus they may be from the time of the temple-tombs of the Héjr merchants—which to guess only after the appearance, might be from the morning of the human world! Monuments of human hands, even ruined graves are a comfortable sight in this Titanic landscape (I, 487).

It cannot be said, of course, that Arabia awakened in him an interest in the beginnings of the human race. Fairley, reviewing Doughty's career as a whole, suggests that all his studies, all his wanderings, whatever digressions might be evident, point to a steadily progressing 'mysterious journey up the wide stream of race and religion that had poured out so much of the life that was in himself and in his beloved country, and was still to pour out for ages to come' (p. 77). But it is certain that Arabia and what he saw there contributed to his interest, and indeed resulted in a deeper realization of the validity of his quest. There is no need to elaborate on the appropriateness of an archaic style to the expression of thoughts and feelings which are elicited by an interest in antiquity. The style of *Arabia Deserta* takes us out of the present into some remote past, and the fact that that style combines, as Miss Treneer has observed, characteristics of 'periods' in English literature usually considered incompatible enhances the effect of timelessness.[29] Doughty's style cannot be dated.

Barker Fairley notes, as we have indicated, that Doughty's archaism is particularly suited to the human ironies of the Arabs' speech. A much less subtle connection between the 'Arab vernacular' and the 'oldest of English prose', he suggests (pp. 20–1), can be illustrated in one example: 'The Red Sea they call simply "The Sea, the Salt Sea:—Zeyd upon a time answered me, when I asked him the sea's name, *Bahr eth Thellam,* "Sea of the glooming (West)."—In like manner our Saxon king, Alfred, in his book of Geography: "Ireland is dim, where the sun goeth on settle."' This is a perfect example of the way in which the Arabs' speech suggested to Doughty the older expressions of English. On another occasion an Arab asked him 'And thy medicines are what? hast thou *tiryák?*' and Doughty observes, 'thus our fathers said treacle, θηριακ-, the antidote of therine poisons' (II, 27). Not only does his style 'reflect several centuries and phases of older English prose because Doughty had travelled back through each of those centuries and phases in order to stand where he stood [at the writing of *Arabia Deserta*]', as Fairley explains (p. 81), but it reflects those older styles also because they were suggested by what he heard with his own ears in Arabia.

7

Thus though he came in contact with only a very small portion of the Middle East, though he certainly did not know the Arabs and their culture so well as did Burton, and though he felt nothing like the sympathy which Blunt felt for the Arabs, Doughty has written a book which far surpasses the work of any writer on Arabia.[30] Basically, the reason for this is that Doughty was in conflict with Arabic culture, in a conflict which arose, strangely enough, from what attracted and repelled him in Arabic culture. He went to Arabia ostensibly to examine inscriptions; but at some time in those first few months of his journey his interest in the past became identified with an interest in the present inhabitants of Arabia, and he decided to live for a time with the nomad natives of that land which perhaps gave birth to humanity. Their way of life, their patterns of thought, and even their language seemed to increase his interest in the origins and development of human society, especially as these pertained to the dawn of civilization in Britain. His historical sense, his patriotism, and his particular brand of Christianity defy separate analyses. Together they form the basis of his spiritual life and the animating force of *Arabia Deserta*. The opposing force in the struggle which is recorded in the book centres about Islam. What Doughty called 'a fanatical religion' had no place in it for a recognition of England as the patron of world morality nor any inclination to accept a liberal Christianity as superior to the religion of God's apostle Mohammed. Whatever Doughty may have known of the theory of Islam, its practice forcefully impressed itself upon him only through his experiences in Arabia. Even though he had no romantic illusions to be dispelled by actual experience, the full realization that the Arabs—living in a land which was sacred to Doughty by virtue of its role in the march of humanity—ignored the prestige of his beloved country and detested its religion could not but cause resentment. Nor must we dismiss lightly the weariness, hunger, and danger which he experienced. Doughty was no ascetic and the sensations of his body had their effects on his thoughts and emotions. Thus, while *Arabia Deserta* records information pertaining to historical research and reflecting Doughty's interest in antiquity, it also records, intermixed in a pattern which imitates the actual experiences of two years in Arabia, the thoughts and emotions of a man torn between feelings of warm humanity and bitter resentment.

But the Doughty who emerged from Arabia was substantially the man who entered it. Nowhere in *Arabia Deserta* is there any indication that he is adding to or modifying his intellectual regimen. The physical hardships he had suffered left their effects on his health, the warm friendships he had made endured in his heart, and experiences—often humiliating and painful—gave him a knowledge of the Arabs and of Arabia; but he never 'warped to Orientalism'. The real significance of *Arabia Deserta* lies not in what Arabia did for Doughty, nor in what Doughty did for Arabia; except that Doughty's sense of the past was deepened, neither, I think, was more than superficially affected by the other. The significance of the book lies rather in its recording of a human struggle against forces which were physically and temperamentally antipathetic.

Whatever important effects his experiences in Arabia had on his sensibilities are recorded in *Arabia Deserta* for all to read. At the end of his experiences he was as proud an Englishman as he was when he began. Fairley's thesis that Doughty's whole life was devoted to his country may be accepted. His studies and his travels can be considered as preparation for his poetry, and his poetry is concerned with England and its origin. This does not mean that *Arabia Deserta* is less significant, for in spite of Doughty's preference for his poetry, the prose work remains his masterpiece. But we must not place too much emphasis on the role of Arabia in Doughty's life and poetry as a whole. The Arabia which influenced Doughty's thought was an Arabia belonging to antiquity. The Near East as the force which influenced Burton and Blunt was repellent to Doughty and could never have exerted a lasting influence on his life.

At any rate, the most important loyalty in Doughty is that to his own race and country. It has been argued that Burton "merged his nationality and abrogated Christianity in the East," and that Blunt was the black sheep of British Imperialism in his espousal of the cause of Eastern freedom from British domination; but Fairley, a very astute critic, has claimed that 'to read the Arabia and then to read *The Character of the Happy Warrior* is to wish to rewrite Wordsworth's Englishman in the light of Doughty'.[31]

V

Doughty, Blunt, and Burton

DOUGHTY, Blunt, and Burton offer interesting contrasts. It would be impossible to measure their respective devotions to England; all were patriotic. But their loyalties are easily differentiated. Doughty was loyal to his race; Blunt was in love with English soil; and Burton gloried in the British Empire. That these differences are not merely accidental, but substantial to an understanding of the sensibilities of the three men, becomes immediately and ludicrously evident if we try to imagine Doughty's saying that conscience is a 'geographical accident' or that Arabia was his 'political first love'—or Blunt's writing that an Arab tribe has a 'rat-like understanding' or that England rules too little and too leniently—or Burton's allowing his beard to be plucked or agitating for Egyptian and Indian independence. Surely, if these men loved England, they loved different things under the same name.

This is partly because England itself was different things, of course—a race devoted to Christian humanitarianism, a land of gentlemen who were polite and sociable, and the mistress of a large portion of the world. But the difference in the loyalties of Doughty, Blunt, and Burton are attributable to the different sensibilities which made them each see and love a different England. Doughty, for all his early desire to follow the sea, was essentially unromantic and could not have been the remarkable traveller-explorer that Burton was. Perhaps the length of *Arabia Deserta* and the two year's period of time which its narrative covers obscure the fact that the geographical area involved is a very small portion of the great Arabian peninsula.

Doughty, Blunt, and Burton

The work, I think, is indicative of the intensity of Doughty's vision. Behind its notebook appearance there is one unifying force: the predisposition of the author to be reminded of antiquity in all that he saw and heard. Someone indeed has quipped (of Doughty's style) that he wrote for antiquity. It would be less clever, but perhaps no less paradoxical in view of the personal experience in *Arabia Deserta*, to say that Doughty wrote *of* antiquity.

But his purpose in writing was to serve his country, to make it more aware of its heritage and its proud origins. His travelling and his studies were calculated to prepare him for service to his race. The languages he learned were related in his linguistic sense to the origins and development of English. He was fired to put life into a language which he thought had atrophied in lifeless Victorian literature. And it is perhaps reasonable to suppose that his intensity of vision subjected his literary ambition to his moral purpose. His prose he considered an apprenticeship to his poetic mission. In *The Cliffs* and *The Clouds* his mission became to warn his countrymen of imminent danger; but his better poetry deals with deeper and more lasting themes: the birth of Christianity in England, the origins of the human race, the riddle of life. Doughty's poetry is at its best when it treats of the past, and even *Arabia Deserta* owes much of its appeal to the way in which it sees through the present and into remote antiquity.

It is sufficiently clear, I think, that Doughty sought in the East the origins of Christianity and humanity. He became involved in Arabia through his desire to investigate inscriptions which he thought might have a biblical significance. Proud of his race and religion, he could not but resent Moslem social and religious prejudices which held England and Christ inferior to the sultan and Mohammed. Thus he remained in conflict with the East, a conflict both physical and spiritual. And the issue was not resolved. Doughty saw in Arabia something, at least, of what he had come to see; and it is substantially true, I think, that the result of his contact with the East was the corroboration of what he already thought and felt. His vision was too intense to be very broad. But the record of his struggle with the East is a monumental piece of literature, because it gives an accurate account of a noble man's conflict with it and

I. BURTON AS A YOUNG MAN.

From *The National Portrait Gallery*, vol. 2, London, 1902.

2. BURTON IN DESERT ROBES.

From *Harper's Magazine*, January 1857.

3. BURTON AS AN OLD MAN.

From *The True Life of Captain Sir Richard F. Burton* by G. Stisted, London, 1896.

4. MR AND LADY BLUNT.
From *Illustrated London News*, 3 March 1888.

5. BLUNT IN DESERT ROBES.

From *A Pilgrimage to Nejd* by Lady Anne Blunt, London, 1881.

6. BLUNT IN A TURBAN.
From *The Bookbuyer*, November 1895.

7. DOUGHTY AS A YOUNG MAN.

From *The Bookman*, June 1927.

8. DOUGHTY AS AN OLD MAN.
From *The Bookman*, March 1926.

its inhabitants. And the author's intensity of vision has a purity which cuts through the ornateness and grotesqueness with which some writers have encumbered the East.

Blunt was much more widely travelled than was Doughty, and his vision was broader. He had a softness of character which made him sensitive to the softness and suffering of others. His was a life of feeling. One after another, emotional experiences occupied his complete attention. He was attracted by the emotional aspects of Catholicism, deeply affected by a passionate love affair, and absorbed by the sense of fulfilment in finding a mission in life in the championing of Arabian independence. Basically he was a country squire in love with the Sussex countryside, and he saw in Arabian tribal life the kind of social structure that appealed to him. He lived the winters as an Arab sheikh, ruling a hundred Arabs and Egyptians and overseeing the work on his oasis. He was drawn into Egyptian politics quite by accident and through his sympathy for the downtrodden peasants. Thus his proper sphere of activity became world politics and he passed through alternate periods of satisfaction and despair.

The East and Blunt helped each other. He was the spokesman for the East in European circles and the East supplied for a time what Blunt had great need of—a direction, or purpose in life. His active crusade did not last; in the end he despaired of Eastern independence from European domination and he was disappointed in his dream of reforming Islam from within. But Blunt had the romantic temperament which enabled him to cling to first loves. He saw in the East romance as well as a practical mission, and when the mission failed him, the romance remained. It was reported that visitors found the old man dozing by the fireplace in his Eastern robes and that he never ceased to be charmed by Arabic literature.

His knowledge of Arabic culture was not so profound as his sympathy with it. His wife was the better Arabist and he based his Eastern poems on her translation of the originals. His versions of the *Golden Odes of Arabia* are true to the spirit of the originals not because he was a great scholar, but because the poems were compatible with his feelings. His *Stealing of the Mare* catches the tone of romanticism that we usually associate with the East, and it makes use of all the ornaments of love in difficulty, the dangerous obstacle to be overcome, the devotion of a fair maiden, and outstanding heroism and chivalry. But though he was most sympathetic with Eastern culture, his rank as a poet must rest on his original love poems, not on his adaptations of Arabic literature. His prose is polemical in nature; even his *Diaries* are calculated to educate the reader in the political importance of the East and the evils of imperialism. His political activities are not so perplexing when we consider that all his political philosophy centred about the principle of local government. He felt that a local government knows the needs of its people, just as a landowner knows the needs of his tenants and so is better able to sympathize with their suffering and act for their good. Thus it is Blunt's capacity for sympathy which is the key to his very Protean activities in general and to his interest in the East in particular.

Burton, too, was sensitive. His *Kasîdah* leaves no doubt of the importance he attached to the emotions; indeed he suspected that the emotions were the only true realities. But Burton's sensitiveness and sympathy were hidden under a hard shell of matter-of-factness. He was a restless wanderer and a quick-witted scholar, but he made his wanderlust serve the practical needs of science and he devoted his scholarship to supplying anthropology with curious information. His *Pilgrimage* and *First Footsteps* are his most readable travel-books largely because he does not burden them with scientific facts. Both are exciting narratives and both reveal the author's sensibilities. In his other travel-books he hides behind a parade of scientific information which was no doubt interesting in the 'sixties and 'seventies, when the earth was still a geographical puzzle not fully solved, but the pieces of information now cease to be intriguing. Thus the books, with little else of interest to offer, suffer the fate of all novelties.

Unlike Blunt's political philosophy which, while unacceptable to his age, is now more sympathetically countenanced, Burton's brand of imperialistic domination by force is now frowned upon. Ironically, it did not endear him to his contemporaries, even at the height of British Imperialism, for he was too obviously ambitious, too undiplomatic in his zeal.

But his edition of the *Arabian Nights* has ensured his popularity. The translation itself is not remarkable except in the boldness of its adherence to the original. Yet the 'anthropological notes' which contribute almost as much as the tales themselves to the common conception and misconception of the East are characteristically Burton's own. Doughty had struggled with the East and Blunt had romantically joined it; Burton seized upon a small portion of its culture, mastered it, and made it subserve his own penchant for the curious and grotesque.

Notes

CHAPTER I

[1] Margaret Cecelia Annan, *The Arabian Nights in Victorian Literature* (Northwestern University Doctoral Dissertation, September, 1945), surveys this field. See also Amy Cruse, *The Victorians and their Reading* (Boston, 1936), pp. 286, 291, and 292, for the place of the *Nights* in the Victorians' reading habits. Miss Annan's dissertation and Marie E. de Meester's 'Oriental Influences in the English Literature of the Nineteenth Century', *Anglistische Forschungen*, Heft 46 (1915), 1–80, should be consulted for a view of the extent and nature of English imitations of Oriental tales in the nineteenth century. Byron Porter Smith, *Islam in English Literature* (Beirut, Lebanon: American Press, 1939), traces changes in the English attitude towards Mohammed until the time of Carlyle.

[2] In addition to *The Travels of Ibn Jubair* William Wright published *A Grammar* of the Arabic Language (2 vols., 1859–62) which was an edited and corrected translation of the German work of Caspari; *Opuscula Arabica* (1859), a collected edition of MSS. in the University Library at Leyden; *The Kamil of Muharrad* (1882); and *The Book of Kalilah and Dimnah* (1883). Besides his translation of the *Arabian Nights*, Edward Lane wrote *An Account of the Manners and Customs of the Modern Egyptians* (2 vols., 1836), *Selections from the Kur'an* (1843), and *An Arabic-English Lexicon* (5 parts, 1863–74). Edward Henry Palmer wrote a treatise on the Sufiistic and Unitarian Theosophy of the Persians, *Oriental Mysticism* (1867); *The Desert of the Exodus* (1871), an account of his journeys undertaken in connection with the English ordnance survey of Sinai; two grammars, *A Grammar of the Arabic Language* (1874), and *The Arabic Manual* (1881); and his translation *The Qur'an* in 1880 as volumes VI and IX in F. Max Muller's *The Sacred Books of the East*. Before publishing the *Two Diwans* already mentioned, Sir Charles James Lyall had written *Translations of Ancient Arabian Poetry, chiefly Prae-Islamic with an Introduction and Notes* (1885); and *Ten Ancient Arabic Poems* (1894).

[3] Unless otherwise noted, the following historical data is drawn from R. C. K. Ensor, *England, 1870–1914* (Oxford, 1936), pp. 40–53; and from George Macaulay Trevelyan, *British History in the Nineteenth Century (1782–1901)* (New York, 1930), pp. 372–88, and 416.

[4] The Earl of Cromer, *Modern Egypt*, 2 vols. (New York, 1908), II, 109, writes: 'The national honour was not to be indefinitely balked of the salve for which it yearned.'

[5] Quoted by John Aberly, *An Outline of Missions* (Philadelphia, 1945),

Notes to pages 5–12

p. 212. The following data on missionary activity are taken from Aberly's work.

[6] The following biographical data, unless otherwise noted, are taken from Mrs. Margaret Oliphant Oliphant, *Memoir of the Life of Laurence Oliphant and of Alice Oliphant, His Wife*, 2 vols. (London, 1891).

[7] This letter is quoted by Mrs. Oliphant, II, 170.

[8] These charges appear in Strachey's *Religious Fanaticism* and are quoted by Herbert W. Schneider and George Lawton, *A Prophet and A Pilgrim* (New York, 1942), p. 376.

[9] The complaints and threats are reported by Schneider, p. 415.

[10] See Isabel Burton, *Life of Sir Richard Burton*, 2 vols. (London, 1893), I, 327–8, and II, 424–5.

[11] See Wilfrid Scawen Blunt, *Secret History of the English Occupation of Egypt. Being a Personal Narrative of Events*, 2nd edition with special appendices (London, 1907), pp. 80, and 87–8.

[12] Reported by D. G. Hogarth, *The Life of Charles M. Doughty* (Oxford, 1928), p. 121.

CHAPTER II

[1] Fairfax Downey, *Burton: Arabian Nights Adventurer* (New York, 1931), p. 12. As the title suggests, this treatment of Burton is in the popular fashion, the purpose being to picture Burton as a character worthy of a place in the *Arabian Nights*. Relying for the most part on Isabel Burton's *Life* (see next note), the author has produced a very readable biography of a fascinating character.

[2] Isabel Burton, *The Life of Captain Sir Richard F. Burton*, 2 vols. (London, 1893), I, 250–5. Somewhat carelessly put together and perhaps too much motivated by the admirable desire to picture Burton as the ideal husband and man, this work is nevertheless a most valuable source for information about Burton. Mrs. Burton quotes extensively from the works of her husband, including those never published, and the opening chapters are devoted to reproducing all of Burton's autobiographical writings. Mrs. Burton, coming from one of England's oldest Roman Catholic families (Arundell), and despite her protestations that she has no motive for so doing, perhaps too ardently tries to show her husband as at least a nominal Catholic. The exotic ancestry hinted at involves a morganatic marriage of Louis XIV, the fact that 'Burton' was the name used by an English tribe of gypsies, and a mere conjecture of some Arab blood somewhere in the distant past of Burton's ancestry. Burton had some of the physical characteristics of the Arab, such as small, finely shaped hands and feet. The following treatment of Burton's early life draws on Isabel Burton's reproduction of her husband's autobiographical writings and her selections from his journals. She destroyed the journals after she had used them in her work.

[3] For the most complete bibliography see Norman M. Penzer, *An Annotated Bibliography of Sir Richard Francis Burton* (London, 1923). The

bibliography in Mrs. Burton's *Life* is not entirely accurate and that in the article on Burton in the *DNB*, XXIII, is not complete.

[4] Captain Sir Richard F. Burton, *Personal Narrative of a Pilgrimage to Al-Madinah & Meccah*, edited by his wife Isabel Burton, with an Introduction by Stanley Lane-Poole, 2 vols. (London, 1907). Original edition published in 1855-6, 3 vols.

[5] Richard F. Burton, *A Plain And Literal Translation Of The Arabian Nights' Entertainments Now Entitled The Book Of The Thousand Nights And A Night With Introduction Explanatory Notes On The Manners And Customs Of Moslem Men And A Terminal Essay Upon The History Of The Nights*, 10 vols. (printed by The Burton Club For Private Subscribers Only, [N.D.]), I, vii–ix. The original volumes were printed between 1885 and 1888. My references to the *Nights* are to a reprint of the original, no date given, but printed between 1900 and 1920.

[6] Anne Treneer, *Charles M. Doughty* (London, 1935), p. 99. Miss Treneer's main concern in this argument seems to be to picture Doughty in as favourable a light as possible. Thus the strictures on Burton are by way of contrast with Doughty.

[7] Achmed Abdullah and Compton T. Pakenham, 'Richard Francis Burton', *Dreamers of Empire* (New York, 1929), p. 58. Abdullah exalts Burton by contrasting him with Doughty.

[8] For example, an Irish Missionary whose opinion was quoted and disparaged by Isabel Burton, I, 179-80.

[9] See Burton's 'Proverbia Communia Syriaca', *Unexplored Syria: Visits To The Libanus, The Tulul El Safa, The Anti-Libanus, The Northern Libanus, And The 'Alah*, 2 vols. (London, 1872), I, Appendix II, 263-5.

[10] Two examples may be found in *Nights*, II, 101, and 108.

[11] See *Pilgrimage*, I, 287. On nearing Medina Burton observes: 'Truly the Arabs show more heart on these occasions than any Oriental people I know; they are of a more affectionate nature than the Persians, and their manners are far more demonstrative than those of the Indians.'

[12] 'Easterns, I have observed, have no way of saying "Thank you"; they express it by a blessing or a short prayer. They have a right to your surplus; daily bread is divided, they say and, eating yours, they consider it their own.' *Nights*, IV, 6. A more detailed defence of the Arab custom is given in *Pilgrimage*, I, 75-7.

[13] Burton felt keenly the tender, true pathos in the following passage, for example: 'When he had ended repeating these verses, he laid his head on his pillow and closed his eyes and slept. Then saw he in his sleep one who said to him, "Rejoice, for thy son shall fill the lands with justest sway; and he shall rule them and him shall the lieges obey." Then he awoke from his dream gladdened by the good tidings he had seen, and after a few days, Death smote him, and because of his dying great grief fell on the people of Baghdad, and simple and gentle mourned for him. But Time passed over him, as though he had never been and Kanmakan's estate was changed; for the people of Baghdad set him aside and put him and his family into a place apart.' *Nights*, III, 55.

[14] See Captain Sir Richard F. Burton, *First Footsteps in East Africa or An*

Exploration of Harar, edited by his wife, Isabel Burton, Memorial Edition, 2 vols. (London, 1894), I, xxx–xxxi. Original edition published in 1856. See also Isabel Burton, I, 114–16.

[15] 'Terminal Essay', *Nights*, X, 65. '... meanwhile, his lively poetic impulse, the poetry of ideas, not the formal verse, and his radiant innate idealism breathe a soul into the merest matter of squalid work-a-day life and awaken the sweetest harmonies of Nature epitomised in Humanity.'

[16] 'The Badawin are not without a certain Platonic affection, which they call Hawá (or *Ishk*) *uzri*—a pardonable love. They draw the fine line between amant and amoureux.' *Pilgrimage*, II, 94.

[17] Richard F. Burton, *The Gold Mines of Midian and The Ruined Midianite Cities. A Fortnight's Tour In North-Western Arabia*, 2nd edition (London, 1878), pp. 154–5. First edition also 1878.

[18] 'I will go still further, and assert that to complete Egypt, Syria should be restored to her. Let me hope that she will soon achieve her independence and express my conviction that when she regains her birthright—Liberty, her progress and development, now arrested only by subjection to Stambúl, will surprise the world.' *Gold Mines*, pp. 21–2.

[19] *Nights*, VIII, 189. These same arguments appear in Burton's 'The Egyptian Question II', *Academy*, XXV (1884), 46. See also his 'England's Duty to Egypt', *Academy*, XXIII (1883), 366, where he argues that now that Egypt is free from Turkey she will be most prosperous under an English Protectorate, 'if only we govern like men, and not like philanthropes and humanitarians'.

[20] *Nights*, IV, 250. However, see V. Lovett Cameron, 'Burton As I Knew Him', *Fortnightly Review*, XIV (1890), 880: 'In his feelings towards the negro race he held a wise position, as far removed, on the one side, from the looking upon each and every man with a dark skin as a "nigger", as from the gushing philanthropy which exalts the negro of the West Coast, debased by gin and spurious civilization, on a pedestal of impossible virtues, on the other ... he was equally strong against forcing upon the negroes a meretricious imitation of European civilization, instead of leading them onwards and upwards to a true civilization of their own. So adverse was he to the results of this spurious culture, that those who did not know the true feelings of the man, when they have read his humorous and cynical remarks upon its unhappy victims, have often considered that he was hostile to them and not to the system of which they are the lamentable results.'

[21] Richard F. Burton, *Supplemental Nights To The Book Of The Thousand Nights and A Night With Notes Anthropological and Explanatory*, 7 vols. (printed by The Burton Club For Private Subscribers Only, [N.D.]), III, 294. However, Burton openly agitates for a strengthening of the abolition of slavery in Egypt in 'England's Duty to Egypt', p. 366. See also V. Lovett Cameron, 'Burton As I Knew Him', p. 880: 'In regard to slavery he was fully in accord with all the best feeling on the subject, and, though he did not enter into the matter actively himself, always encouraged me in my endeavours to combat this evil, and gave me good and wholesome advice, which moreover had the advantage of being practical and practicable.'

[22] *Nights*, VI, 54. Some biographers of Burton would consider the passage

as an example of Burton's habit of posing. See, for example, Ouida (Madame Ramée), 'Richard Burton', *Fortnightly Review*, LXXXV (1906), 1040–1: 'Besides, to the difficulties which his character offered to any comprehension by the ordinary man there was added the delight he took in mystifying people, in terrifying them, in painting himself as the devil before the frightened eyes of timid mortals.'

[23] See, for example, the official letter to Burton from H. L. Anderson, Secretary to Government, Bombay, July 23, 1857, reprinted in Isabel Burton, *Life*, II, 565. See also Downey, pp. 285–6. An anonymous reviewer of Isabel Burton's *Life* in *Edinburgh Review*, CLXXVIII (1893), 440–1, writes that Burton failed to be a success either as a soldier, diplomat, or explorer because his superiors never knew what dependence could be placed on him, because they 'were never sure that at some crucial moment he might prefer his own opinion to their order'. His lack of success was due, the reviewer adds, 'largely also to the insolent want of tact of which he was frequently guilty, and that not only in official but in social matters, when it took a more offensive form'.

[24] 'Terminal Essay', *Nights*, X, 205–6. William Henry Wilkins, *The Romance of Isabel Lady Burton; The Story of Her Life* (London, 1898), pp. 729–31, is sure that this is the reason for Burton's failure to rise in the consular service.

[25] Downey, *Burton*, p. 195. For other apologies, see Wilkins, *Romance*, p. 729: Burton's 'anthropological interest' was 'ethnological and historical'; Cameron, 'Burton', p. 881: 'As the pathologist must study pathology in order to find a cure for disease, so Burton, as a student of human nature, had to examine and analyse the impure as well as the pure, for human nature is so intimately compounded of both good and evil that he who studies one alone is apt to arrive at conclusions more erroneous than he would if he had never studied at all'; and Frank Harris, 'Sir Richard Burton', II, *Academy*, LXXXI (1911), 390: 'He told me (what I had already guessed) that the freedom of speech he used, he used deliberately, not to shock England but to teach England that only by absolute freedom of speech and thought could she ever come to be worthy of her heritage.'

[26] 'Introduction' to *Pilgrimage*, I, xix–xx. The reviewer of Lady Burton's *Life*, in the *Edinburgh Review*, CLXXVIII (1893), 467, calls the *Nights* 'one of the most indecent books in the English language' and justly observes that offensive matter is brought in often '*à propos de bottes*' in a footnote.

[27] *Supplemental Nights*, VII, 385. ' "It has occurred to me that perhaps it would be a good plan to put a set of notes ... to the 'Origin', which now has none, exclusively devoted to the errors of my reviewers. It has occurred to me that where a reviewer has erred, a common reader might err. Secondly, it will show the reader that we must not trust implicitly to reviewers."—Darwin's Life, ii, 349.'

[28] *Nights*, III, 213. See 'Terminal Essay', *Nights*, X, 192–202, for a detailed discussion of the role played by women in the *Nights*.

[29] For a good example, see *Nights*, VII, 371: 'But the Moslems were animated with an ardent love of liberty and Kufah under Al-Hajjaj the masterful, lost 100,000 of her turbulent sons without the thirst for indepen-

dence being quenched. This can hardly be said of the Early Christians, who, with the exception of a few staunch martyrs, appear in history as pauvres diables and poules mouillées, ever oppressed by their own most ignorant and harmful fancy that the world was about to end.'

[30] From journals quoted by Isabel Burton, I, 103.

[31] From journals quoted by Isabel Burton, I, 123. In the autobiography written for Hitchman in 1888, reprinted in Isabel Burton's *Life*, I, 135, the incident is tied in with Burton's study of the *Bubu* system; i.e. the system of having a native woman rather than an English wife. With this system, of course, the 'Portuguese *padre*' was not in sympathy, and Burton proved to be a painful charge to the priest.

[32] Isabel Burton, I, 123, footnote. The controversy centres about the very dramatic death scene. Lady Burton describes the scene in volume II, 410–14: she reports that her husband was alive but insensible when she had the priest administer the Roman Catholic Sacrament of Extreme Unction. However, Georgiana Stisted, *The True Life of Capt. Sir Richard F. Burton*, With The Authority And Approval of The Burton Family (London, 1896), pp. 409–414, claims that Burton was already dead, and ridicules the Catholic rites and ceremonies insisted upon by Lady Burton. It is significant, perhaps, that Burton's niece, Miss Stisted, wrote after the death of Lady Burton, and that she was intensely anti-Catholic. The physician who was the constant companion of Burton during the last three and a half years of Burton's life, and who was present when Burton died, is silent on the issue: see Dr. F. Crenfell Baker, 'Sir Richard Burton As I Knew Him', *Cornhill Magazine*, New Series, LI (1921), 411–23. Achmed Abdullah, 'Richard Francis Burton', pp. 90–107, follows the lead of Miss Stisted as does Ouida, 'Richard Burton', *Fortnightly Review*, LXXXV (1906), 1043: 'I know not what others may think of this act; to me it was an unpardonable treachery.' Thomas Wright, *The Life of Sir Richard Burton*, 2 vols. (London, 1906), II, 240, claims that Burton was 'dead but warm'. Wilkins, *Romance of Lady Isabel Burton*, pp. 713–15, meets Miss Stisted's charges systematically and concludes that Lady Burton's account is the more credible.

[33] Sir Richard Francis Burton, *The Kasîdah of Haji Abdu El-Yezdi* (Portland, Maine, 1911), p. 67. Original edition published in 1880.

[34] *First Footsteps*, I, 108.

[35] A. Symons, 'Neglected and Mysterious Genius', *Forum*, LXVII (1922), 246: 'Burton's face has no actual beauty in it, it reveals a tremendous animalism, an air of repressed ferocity, a devilish fascination. There is almost a tortured magnificence in this huge head; tragic and painful, with its mouth that aches with desire; with those dilated nostrils that drink in I know not what strange perfumes.'

[36] Character portrayals of Burton are quite varied: Cameron, 'Burton As I Knew Him', p. 879, writes that 'under the rugged exterior there was a heart as tender as that of any woman'. (Cameron was Burton's companion on the trip which is described in *To The Gold Coast For Gold*.) Harris, 'Sir Richard Burton', Part II, p. 390, holds that 'In spite of his talent for literature, in spite of his extraordinary gift of speech, Burton was at bottom a man of action, a great leader, a still greater governor of men.' Symons, 'Neglected

and Mysterious Genius', p. 239, writes that Burton 'was a mixture of the normal and the abnormal; he was perverse and passionate; he was imaginative and cruel; he was easily stirred to rage'. The anonymous writer of 'Eminent un-Victorian', *Living Age*, CCCIX (1921), 296, says, 'His energy was on the engine rather than the human plan. He went through a new language or other field of facts like a reaping machine. His temperament was pure Renaissance. The demon of curiosity drove him about the world insatiable of knowledge and experience.' The anonymous reviewer of Lady Burton's *Life*, *Edinburgh Review*, CLXXVIII (1893), 443, indicates that the key to understanding Burton's character is the realization that 'the boy became a man without the most elementary notions of discipline and obedience'. And Dr. Baker, 'Burton As I Knew Him', *Cornhill Magazine*, New Series, LI (1921), 411, thinks that interest in Burton will always be due to 'the atmosphere of chivalrous and single-minded romanticism that ever surrounded his exceptionally virile and human personality in all he did throughout his life'.

[37] Harris, 'Sir Richard Burton', Part II, p. 391, emphasizes this point: 'A child of the mystical East, a master of Semitic thought which has produced the greatest religions, Burton was astoundingly matter-of-fact. There was no touch of the visionary in him——'

[38] Harris, 'Sir Richard Burton', Part I, p. 363: 'His ethnological appetite for curious customs and crimes, for everything singular and savage in humanity was insatiable. A Western American lynching yarn held him spellbound; a *crime passionel* in Paris intoxicated him, started him talking, transfiguring him into a magnificent storyteller, with intermingled appeal of pathos and rollicking fun, camp-fire effects, jets of flame against the night.'

[39] Symons, 'Neglected and Mysterious Genius', p. 235, admits 'he was a man of genius; only, the fact is he was not a great writer'. Anon., 'Eminent un-Victorian', p. 297, criticizes the *Pilgrimage* for its 'levelness of recital which brings the more momentous passages upon the reader suddenly as if he had collided with someone in turning a corner'. H. J. Cook, 'Review of The *Kasidah*', *Athenaeum*, No. 3799 (August 18, 1900), 216, claims that Burton did not have 'the delicacy of ear and distinction of style which are the poet's incommunicable gift'. But he finds that there is eloquence and vigour and that 'in descriptive passages many a felicitous touch causes regret that Sir Richard should have devoted so little space to the magic and mystery of the desert'.

[40] A contemporary review, Andrew Wilson, 'Review of *Gold Mines of Midian*', *Academy*, XIV (1878), 129, notes the change in style and estimates that 'it is not so much that Captain Burton's hand has lost its cunning as that his will has made what we deem an erroneous choice'.

[41] Harris, 'Sir Richard Burton', Part I, p. 363, reports that 'Burton's laughter, even, deep chested as it was, had in it something of sadness'.

CHAPTER III

[1] The description of this episode and Blunt's criticism of Burton are part of the entry for March 18, 1906, in Wilfrid Scawen Blunt, *My Diaries: Being a Personal Narrative of Events 1888–1914*, 2 vols. (New York, 1922), II, 128–32. This work was first published in London, 1919–20, also in 2 vols. There is also a one volume edition, London, 1932. Unless otherwise noted, all quotations and data in this chapter are derived from this work.

[2] Edith Finch, in *Wilfrid Scawen Blunt* (London, 1938), pp. 51–2, thinks Blunt was under Burton's influence at Buenos Aires. She illustrates her opinion by repeating gossip about Blunt's riding out on a dark night to keep a tryst with a rancher's wife, of the rancher's unexpected return, a narrow escape, etc. Miss Finch's book is an excellent biography of Blunt.

[3] Quoted by Edith Finch, p. 339. Most critics of Blunt agree on the sincerity of his poetry; for example, Samuel C. Chew, 'Wilfrid Scawen Blunt: Self-Determinist', *New Republic*, XXIII (1920), 250, calls it 'the Byronic tradition in his poetry'; John F. Fenlon, D.D., 'Wilfrid Scawen Blunt', *Catholic World*, CXVI (1922), 359, thinks that Blunt acquired Rousseau's 'concentration of self', and that 'Blunt had no genius, not enough imagination to deal easily with any topic but himself'; Desmond MacCarthy, 'Wilfrid Blunt', *Portraits* (New York, 1932), p. 33, is certain that 'those who value poetry as a medium for the expression of life [rather than "poetry of art"] will not forget the poems of Wilfrid Blunt'; and Percy Addleshaw, 'Mr. Wilfrid Blunt's Poetry', *National Review* (1897), 206, wrote that it is the 'strong personal note' which is the chief virtue of most of Blunt's poetry and the greatest defect in *In Vinculis* and in *The Wind and The Whirlwind*.

[4] The biographical data in this section, unless otherwise noted, are derived from Edith Finch, *Wilfrid Scawen Blunt*.

[5] Wilfrid Scawen Blunt, *Secret History of the English Occupation of Egypt. Being A Personal Narrative of Events*, 2nd edition with special appendices (London, 1907), p. 1.

[6] Edith Finch, p. 6.

[7] *Secret History*, p. 3.

[8] For an idyllic picture of Blunt's life at Sheykh Obeyd see Frederic Harrison, *Autobiographical Memoirs*, 2 vols. (London, 1911), II, 173–9. 'I found our Sheik's name a passport everywhere... We passed through the grove of palms, under which a score of Arab mares were tethered, and at the rude stone outer gate the Nubian janissary said to me, "El Sheikh!" and there, sure enough, was Wilfrid, in an immense white burnous, white baggy trousers, and an Arab—not Turkish—white head-dress and lapels—like the Sultan of Morocco' (175).

[9] Wilfrid Scawen Blunt, *In Vinculis* (London, 1889), pp. 9–10.

[10] Wilfrid Scawen Blunt, 'Quatrains of Life', *The Poetical Works. A Complete Edition*, 2 vols. (London, 1914), I, 416. Subsequent references in connection with Blunt's poetry will be to this edition of his verse, unless otherwise indicated.

[11] *My Diaries*, II, 42–3. Blunt's unqualified praise of pre-Islamic poetry is

found in 'Arabian Poetry of the Days of Ignorance', *The New Review*, XIV (1896), 626-35, where he extols the hedonistic and uninhibited Arabs of the desert.

[12] Wilfrid Scawen Blunt and Dr. Charles Meynell, *Proteus and Amadeus: A Correspondence*, ed. by Aubrey de Vere (London, 1878), p. 24. The book was published without the authors' names and some attempt was made to conceal their identity by the substitution of fictitious names for such places and persons as Stonyhurst, Oscott, Fr. Porter, etc.

[13] Quoted by Edith Finch, p. 47.

[14] *My Diaries*, II, 246-7. This is the type of hint, and there are not very many in all, which Blunt makes in his *Diaries* about his relations with women. The purpose of the *Diaries*, of course, is political. The following paragraph from Edith Finch, p. 266, concerning Blunt's relations with women, and especially after his release from prison, is enough to fill the gaps in the *Diaries*: 'To his women friends Blunt found that his prison adventures had become a title to romantic interest, which made it easy for him to resume his place in society. Blunt's relations with women form the background of his life from first to last and for obvious reasons were highly important to him during this period of rehabilitation. He was fastidious and not exceptionally passionate, but love affairs were part of the social game in which his charm and good looks gave him the advantage. Victory won, his vanity was satisfied and lasting friendship was often the result.'

[15] Quotations and data concerning Blunt's acquaintance with Eastern politics are drawn from his *Secret History*.

[16] Wilfrid Scawen Blunt, *The Future of Islam* (London, 1882), pp. 6-7. The following account of Blunt's espousal of the cause of Islam is based on this work.

[17] E. M. Forster, *Abinger Harvest* (New York, 1936), p. 282.

[18] *My Diaries*, II, 148.

[19] Wilfrid Scawen Blunt, *Atrocities of Justice under British Rule in Egypt* (London, 1906), pp. 3-4.

[20] *Atrocities of Justice*, pp. 6-7.

[21] *Atrocities of Justice*, pp. 60-3.

[22] *My Diaries*, I, 321. The Dervishes were slaughtered in the battle at Omdurman in the Soudan in October, 1898. See Evelyn Baring, First Earl of Cromer, *Modern Egypt*, 2 vols. (New York, 1908), II, 109-10, for the imperialistic view of the affair. Public opinion was clamouring for the revenge of Gordon.

[23] See *My Diaries*, I, 22. He ascribed other reasons as well: 'an intimacy which I then for the first time enjoyed with William Morris', which confirmed him in his resolution to 'retire into my shell' politically (*My Diaries*, I, 23, and 25); and his disappointment about Egypt in the following year which turned him back 'with redoubled zest' to his social pleasures of the year before (*My Diaries*, I, 53).

[24] *My Diaries*, II, 114. He had always shown a predisposition towards religious ceremony. Fifteen years before he declared his love for 'old Mosaic rites and superstitions' in his report of activities at Sheykh Obeyd: *My Diaries*, I, 15.

²⁵ Edith Finch, pp. 354-5.
²⁶ Quoted by Edith Finch, p. 353.
²⁷ Edith Finch, pp. 353-4.
²⁸ Edith Finch, p. 371, quotes some of the directions for his burial found in his will. She seems sceptical about the sincerity of Blunt's acceptance of the last rites of the Catholic Church.
²⁹ R. B. Cunninghame Graham, 'Wilfrid Scawen Blunt', *English Review*, XXV (1922), 487.
³⁰ For examples, Graham, 489, calls him 'a super-tramp, taking the whole world as his beat'; Francis Toye, 'An English Don Quixote', *English Review*, LV (1932), 559, writes that 'he was essentially Don Quixote reincarnated in an English gentleman of the nineteenth century. His windmills were, in the abstract, Imperialism and International Finance; in the concrete, Cecil Rhodes and Lord Cromer. Where they were concerned he was a fanatic'; John F. Fenlon, D.D., 'Wilfrid Scawen Blunt', *Catholic World*, CXVI (1922), 369, thought that 'modern history shows no sadder example of a man without God and hope in the world'; Sister Mary Joan Reinehr, *The Writings of Wilfrid Scawen Blunt* (Milwaukee, Wisconsin, 1940), p. 1, writes that 'Blunt's romantic soul sought continually for the abundant life and found complete satisfaction only in energetic action'; and E. M. Forster, *Abinger Harvest* p. 279, observes, 'He was sensitive, enthusiastic, and sincere, but he had not within him the fiery whirlwind that transcends a man's attitude, and sweeps him, whatever his opinions, into the region where acts and words become eternal. His life, like his poetry, lacked this supreme quality.'
³¹ See Edith Finch, pp. 355-6. She writes that 'his kindness, like that of most really kind people not worn on his sleeve, sprang from a sensitive imagination as much as from intention. He understood the traditions and individual foibles of both tenants and servants, respected their special knowledge, found interest and amusement in their shrewd talk.'
³² But he loved Arabic. Padraic Colum, 'Wilfrid Scawen Blunt', *Commonweal*, XIV (1931), 636, writes that once after reciting some Arabic poetry Blunt said, 'Arabic is a language to be shouted across great spaces—a language of the open air and the desert.' Shane Leslie, 'Wilfrid Blunt', *Men Were Different* (London, 1937), p. 259, says Blunt was very susceptible to flattery on his Arabic.
³³ Shane Leslie writes: 'His love for the Arabs was the love of his life' (p. 237) and 'In the end Islam proved the supreme disappointment of his thwarted life' (p. 229).

CHAPTER IV

¹ Quoted by Anne Treneer, *Charles M. Doughty* (London, 1935), p. 392.
² See D. G. Hogarth, *The Life of Charles M. Doughty* (Oxford, 1928), p. 127.
³ Wilfrid Scawen Blunt, *My Diaries*, 2 vols. (New York, 1922), I, 273.
⁴ Reported by Samuel C. Chew, 'Wilfrid Scawen Blunt: An Intimate View', *The North American Review*, CCXVII (1923), 667.

⁵ Edith Finch, *Wilfrid Scawen Blunt* (London, 1938), p. 338.

⁶ Richard F. Burton, 'Mr. Doughty's Travels in Arabia', *Academy*, XXXIV (July 28, 1888), 47–8.

⁷ The biographical and bibliographical data in the following pages are taken from Hogarth. Hogarth was requested by Mrs. Doughty to write the biography of her husband and unpublished material, especially letters, as well as reminiscences of members of the family and friends were made available to him. He himself had some correspondence with Doughty.

⁸ Barker Fairley, *Charles M. Doughty: A critical Study*, (London, 1927), p. 9.

⁹ Quoted by Hogarth, p. 173. Fairley, pp. 183–4, thinks that the cause of the failure of *The Cliffs* and *The Clouds* was Doughty's abandonment of 'the scholarly and scientific instincts that were rooted in him' and which had guided his choice of subject matter in his other poetry. John Holloway, 'Poetry and Plain Language: The Verse of C. M. Doughty', *Essays in Criticism*, IV (January, 1954), 67, thinks that these same two poems fail because they have their source not in Doughty's vital experience but in his anxiety.

¹⁰ These quotations are in Hogarth, p. 191.

¹¹ Holloway in his recent article, p. 58, defends Doughty's style against the charge of Gerard Manley Hopkins that Doughty's archaism is unmanly and insincere.

¹² But Martin Armstrong, 'Charles Doughty', *The North American Review*, CCXIV (1921), 260, thinks that 'since his [Doughty's] poetical style is an intensification of his prose, it is perhaps not idle to say that his poetry has grown directly out of the great spiritual experience of *Arabia Deserta*'. An anonymous critic in 'Charles Montagu Doughty', *The Times Literary Supplement*, XXV (February 11, 1926), 86, laments that *Adam Cast Forth* was not Doughty's epic poem, for he finds it 'intense and sublime, written out of the knowledge of one who had been driven from oasis into desert and stumbled back into earthly Eden again'. He calls the poem (p. 85) 'a sublime simplification of all that he lived and learned in the Arabian Desert'.

¹³ T. E. Lawrence, 'Introduction' to Charles M. Doughty, *Arabia Deserta*, new and definitive edition in one volume (New York: Random House [N.D.]), I, 17. My references will be to this edition, the pagination of which assumes two volumes. The book was first published by the Cambridge University Press, 2 vols., 1888; by Philip Lee Warner, Publisher to the Medici Society, Ltd., and Jonathan Cape, with a new preface by the author and an introduction by T. E. Lawrence, 2 vols., 1921; by the Medici Society and Jonathan Cape, with a third preface by the author and without the introduction by T. E. Lawrence, 2 vols., 1923; and by Jonathan Cape and the Medici Society, with the third preface by the author and the introduction by T. E. Lawrence, one volume thin paper edition, 1926.

¹⁴ Fairley, p. 79.

¹⁵ Miss Treneer, p. 19, observes that Doughty was a 'very son of the Renaissance' in his 'instinct for direct examination of natural phenomena' and in his 'enthusiasm for his country and his fervour'.

¹⁶ Fairley, p. 46, makes this observation.

¹⁷ Lawrence, pp. 23–4. And Martin Armstrong, 'The Works of Charles

Doughty', *Fortnightly Review*, CXXV (1926), 24, writes that 'if the object of a book of travels is to give a vivid and complete impression of the country and its inhabitants, an impression not modified or limited by the prejudices and partialities of the traveller, then this book of Doughty's achieves the ideal'.

[18] Lawrence, p. 19. But John Middleton Murry, 'Arabia Deserta', *The Adelphi*, III (March, 1926), 660, writes: 'Such was the man who measured himself with unknown Arabia—a man of higher and more enlightened tradition, but of a like basic fanaticism [with the Arabs].'

[19] Fairley, 28-9. Miss Treneer, p. 96, thinks that it is partly because of Doughty's 'very unlikeness to his hosts and his stiff-neckedness in preserving that unlikeness' that he was able to mingle as freely with the Arabs as he did.

[20] Burton, 'Mr. Doughty's Travels', p. 48.

[21] Achmed Abdullah and Compton T. Pakenham, 'Richard Francis Burton', *Dreamers of Empire* (New York, 1929), p. 57.

[22] Roberts is quoted by Miss Treneer, p. 99.

[23] Miss Treneer, p. 259, reports that in a letter to Edward Garnett in 1909 Doughty expressed the opinion that Humanity was the ultimate religion of man but that perhaps millenniums must pass before its realization. And Martin Armstrong in *The North American Review*, p. 266, writes: 'Doughty is a Christian. He accepts Christ as his guide along the path of human goodness. He has a great capacity for veneration and fine emotion, so that, as regards ultimate things, his religion is, I think, free from dogmas,—the serene aspiration of a golden temperament . . . meekly adoring the Eternal Verities.'

[24] *Arabia Deserta*, I, 599. But the anonymous critic of Doughty in *The Times Literary Supplement*, XXV (February 11, 1926), 85, thinks that '. . . if Doughty could have had his way, he would have replaced democracy by something worse—a rigid and tyrannous theocracy. For in his imagination God and England were one, precisely as God and Israel were one to the Jews of old; and in "The Cliffs" (1909) he pushes his idea relentlessly to the point of savagery. In that poem the image of 'Sancta Britannia' is precisely as the idol of a savage tribe. . . .'

[25] Fairley, p. 186. See also page 184, where he constructs an apology for the failures, *The Cliffs* and *The Clouds*, on the basis of Doughty's patriotism. The critic in *The Times Literary Supplement*, XXV (February 11, 1926), 85, holds that 'Doughty's poetry, in conception and in diction, is the poetry of a fanatic' and that 'from beginning to end, save for one remarkable exception [*Adam Cast Forth*], it is warped'.

[26] *Arabia Deserta*, I, 592. Miss Treneer, pp. 16-17, maintains that Doughty 'stud[ied] words no less as a moralist than as a poet, believing that the right use of vital language was essential to the health of individuals and nations'.

[27] Doughty expresses these views in two letters to Hogarth. The biographer quotes from them on pages 11 and 12.

[28] Fairley, p. 82. See also his prefatory note, p. 25, in which he explains that he did not learn, until the final stages of his writing, that Doughty had indicated having the idea of *The Dawn in Britain* in his mind before his Arabian travels. Walt Taylor, 'Doughty's English', *Society For Pure English*,

Tract LI (1939), 3–41, looks upon Doughty's travels throughout Europe and the Middle East as a pilgrimage to the sources of the English language.

[29] Treneer, p. 127. Walt Taylor, p. 3, writes: 'Doughty's style was at once modern, Chaucerian and Arabic; its Chaucerian and Elizabethan quality is no mere pastiche; it is Arabic; it is "pure" English written by a modern writer of genius.'

[30] Samuel C. Chew, 'The Poetry of Charles Montague Doughty', *The North American Review*, CCXXII (1925), 292, writes that 'considered more broadly, Doughty's work might serve as the culmination of the entire history of the influence of the Levant upon English literature'.

[31] Fairley, p. 76. An editorial on Doughty in *The London Mercury*, XIII (February, 1926), 338, contains the following supreme praise of Doughty and *Arabia Deserta*: 'It would be difficult to do justice to the magnificence of that book. It is the work of a scholar, a hero and a saint.'

Index

Abdullah, Achmed, 18, 22, 117, 140[7], 143[32], 149[21]
Aberly, John, 138[5]
Addleshaw, Percy, 145[3]
Anderson, H. L., 142[23]
Annan, Margaret Cecelia, 138[1]
Arabi Pasha, 3, 56
Armstrong, Martin, 148[12], 149[23]
Augustine, 48
Austin, Alfred, 82, 88

Bacon, Francis, 47
Baker, Dr. F. Crenfell, 143[32], 144[36]
Barry, Father Angelo de, 68
Bartema, Lodovico, 13
Beaumont, Frederica, 97
Bell, Gertrude, 5
Belloc, Hilaire, 92
Berkeley, George, 47
Berlin, Congress of, 3, 82
Blunt, Lady Anne Noel, 57, 59, 60, 76, 78, 135
Blunt, Wilfrid Scawen, vii, viii, 53–94, 145–7; association with Burton, 53–5; biography, 56–60; sensitivity and capacity for sympathy, 60–71; religious difficulties, 71–4; his interest in the East, 74–84; last years, 84–92; character sketch, 93–4; association with Laurence Oliphant, 7–8; association with Doughty, 95–6; compared and contrasted with Burton and Doughty, 133–7; *Atrocities of Justice Under British Rule in Egypt*, 60, 81, 146[19], [20], [21]; *The Bride of the Nile*, 59; *Esther*, 59, 91; *Fand of the Fair Cheek*, 59; *The Future of Islam*, 58, 79–80, 85–6, 146[16]; *Gordon at Khartoum*, 60; *Griselda*, 59; *Ideas About India*, 58; *India Under Ripon*, 60; *In Vinculis*, 59, 145[9]; *The Land War in Ireland*, 55–6, 59, 60; *The Little Left Hand*, 59; 'Love Lyrics', 59; *Love Sonnets of Proteus*, 58, 91; *The Mu'allakat or Seven Golden Odes of Arabia*, 55, 59, 93, 135; *My Diaries*, 53–4, 60–91 *passim*, 136, 145[1, 11], 146[14, 18, 22-4], 147[3]; 'Natalia's Resurrection', 59; *A New Pilgrimage*, 58; *The Poetical Works, A Complete Edition*, 60; *Proteus and Amadeus: A Correspondence*, 66–73 *passim*, 146[12]; 'Quatrains of Life', 66, 68, 72–3, 91; *Religion of Happiness*, 92; *Satan Absolved*, 56, 59; *Secret History of the English Occupation of Egypt*, 60, 74–7, 78, 85, 139[11], 145[5, 7], 146[15]; 'Sed Nos Qui Vivimus', 74, 86; *Songs and Sonnets by Proteus*, 58; *The Stealing of the Mare*, 56, 59, 93, 135; *The Wind and the Whirlwind*, 56, 58, 59
Boccaccio, 21
Boers, 82, 101
Bonaparte, Napoleon, 27
Bonney, T. G., 98
Bourke, Terence, 87
Browne, Edward G., 5
Burckhardt, John Lewis, 13
Burne-Jones, Edward, 95

Index

Burton, Lady Isabel, 7–8, 9, 44, 47, 139[1, 2, 10], 140[8], 142[23], 143[30, 31, 32], 144[36]

Burton, Richard Francis, vii–viii, 9–52, 139–45; early life, 9–11; bibliography, 12; interest in travel, 5, 13–17, 100; patriotism, 17–31; 'anthropological' interest, 31–8; his understanding of Moslems, 38–43, 109; his philosophy, 43–9; character sketch, 49–52; association with Laurence Oliphant, 7–8; association with Wilfrid Scawen Blunt, 53; review of *Arabia Deserta*, 96; compared and contrasted with Blunt and Doughty, 133–7; as 'F. B.' (Frank Baker), 44; *Arabian Nights Entertainments*, viii, 2, 8, 12, 17, 22–52 *passim*, 136–7, 140[5, 10], 141[19, 20, 22], 142[24, 27, 28, 29]; *The City of Saints*, 12, 51; *First Footsteps in East Africa*, 24–5, 27, 29, 43, 51, 52, 136, 140–1[14], 143[34]; *The Gold Mines of Midian*, 17, 27, 29, 52, 141[17, 18]; *The Highlands of Brazil*, 12; *The Kasîdah*, 12, 44–9, 51, 52, 136, 143[33]; *Lake Regions of Central Africa*, 51; *The Lusiads of Camoens*, 51; *Midian Revisited*, 17; *Paraguay*, 12; *Pilgrimage to Al-Madinah & Meccah*, 12, 13–21, 26, 28, 51, 52, 136, 140[4, 11], 141[16], 142[26]; *Sind Revisited*, 12; *Supplemental Nights*, 32–7, 141[21]; *To the Gold Coast for Gold*, 12, 51; *Ultima Thule*, 12; *Unexplored Syria*, 51–2, 140[9]

Byron, Lord, 69, 78

Camberwell Elections, 58
Cameron, Captain George Poulett, 78, 142[25], 143[36]
Cape, Jonathan, 148[13]
Carlyle, Thomas, 1
Caspari, 138[2]
Cavaliere, Signor, 98–9
Chaucer, 100, 104
Chew, Samuel C., 145[3], 147[4], 150[30]
Church Missionary Society, 5

Cobden, Richard, 25–6
Colum, Padraic, 147[32]
Cook, H. J., 144[39]
Crabbet Estates, 57, 76, 93
Crimean War, 3, 122
Cromer, Lord Evelyn Baring, 3–4, 58, 59, 63, 81–2, 138[4], 147[30]
Cruse, Amy, 138[1]
Currie, Mary, 68
Curzon, Robert, 5
Cuthbert, Father, 68

Dante, 39
Darwin, Charles, 32, 72, 83
Denshawai Case, 81
Deptford Elections, 59, 79
Disraeli, Benjamin, 3, 82
Doughty, Rev. Charles Montagu, 97
Doughty, Charles Montagu, vii, viii, 95–132; criticism by Burton and Blunt, 95–6; biographical sketch, 97–102; knowledge of the Arabs, 102–9; friendliness with the Arabs, 109–13; lack of sympathy with the Arabs, 113–21; struggle with the Arabs, 121–30; character sketch, 130–2; association with Laurence Oliphant, 7–8; compared and contrasted with Burton and Blunt, 133–7; *Adam Cast Forth*, 101, 102; *Arabia Deserta*, viii, 8, 95–134 *passim*; *The Cliffs*, 101; *The Clouds*, 101; *The Dawn in Britain*, 101; *Documents épigraphiques recueillis dans le nord de l'Arabie*, 100; *On the Joestedal-brae Glaciers in Norway*, 97; *Mansoul or the Riddle of the World*, 101–2; *The Titans*, 101; *Under Arms*, 101
Downey, Fairfax, 9, 31, 139[1], 142[25]

East India Company, 17
Echo, 33, 35
Edinburgh Review, 33, 36
Ensor, R. C. K., 138[3]
Erasmus, Desiderius, 98
Euphrates Valley Railroad, 78

Index

Fairley, Barker, 100, 102, 103, 114, 123, 125, 128, 129–30, 131, 132, 148[8, 9, 14, 16], 149[19, 25, 28], 150[31]
F. B. (Frank Baker), *see* Burton, Richard
Fenlon, John F., 145[3], 147[30]
Fernando, Don, 70
Finati, Giovanni, 13
Finch, Edith, 66, 68, 69, 70, 71, 92, 145[2, 3, 4, 6], 146[13], 147[25, 26, 27, 28, 31], 148[5]
Forster, E. M., 80–1, 146[17], 147[30]
Frere, Sir Bartle, 77

Galland, Antoine, 2
Galloway, Lady, 64
Garnett, Edward, 101, 102, 149[23]
Gerard, Father, 60
Gladstone, William Ewart, 3–4
Gordon, General Charles George, 4, 83, 146[22]
Graham, R. B. Cunninghame, 92, 147[29, 30]
Gregory, Lady Augusta, 55
Grey, Sir Edward, 81

Haeckel, Ernst Heinrich, 72
Hankey, Frederick, 47
Harris, Frank, 142[25], 143[36], 144[37, 38, 41]
Harris, Thomas Lake, 6–7
Harrison, Frederick, 145[8]
Henley, William Ernest, 64
Hitchman, Francis, 44, 143[31]
Hogarth, David G., 5, 101, 139[12], 147[2], 148[7, 9, 10], 149[27]
Holloway, John, 148[9, 11]
Holywell, 88–9
Homer, 21
Hopkins, Gerard Manley, 148[11]
Hotham, Hon. and Rev. Frederick, 97
Hunt, Dr. James, 38
Huxley, Thomas Henry, 67

Jameson, Dr. (Sir Leander Starr), 82

Kidderminster Elections, 58

Kinglake, Alexander William, 5
Kipling, Rudyard, 92
Kitchener, Sir Herbert, 4

Lamarck, 45
Lane, Edward William, 2, 138[1]
Lane-Poole, Stanley, 2, 16–17, 18–19, 31–2, 33, 36, 140[4]
Laprimaudaye, Annie, 68
Lawrence, Thomas Edward, 102, 103, 105, 109–10, 121, 148[13], 148–9[17], 149[18]
Lawton, George, 139[8]
Layard, Sir Austin Henry, 5
Leo, Pope XIII, 67
Leslie, Shane, 147[32, 33]
Le Strange, Alice, 6–7
Leutwein, Helen, 69, 71
Locke, John, 48
Lyall, Sir Alfred, 77
Lyall, Sir Charles James, 2, 138[2]
Lytton, Lord ('Owen Meredith'), 57, 58, 70, 76–7

MacCarthy, Desmond, 145[3]
Malet, Lady, 75
Meester, Marie E. de, 138[1]
Meynell, Dr. Charles, 66–7, 71–2, 85, 146[12]
Mill, John Stuart, 67
Mivart, Dr., 68
Morris, William, 95, 146[23]
Muller, F. Max, 138[2]
Murry, John Middleton, 149[18]

Newman, Francis W., 48
Newman, John Henry Cardinal, 1, 11, 48–9, 50
Noel, Edward, 69
Noel, Lady Anne, *see* Blunt, Lady Anne Noel
Novalis, 45

Oliphant, Laurence, 5–8, 139[8]
Oliphant, Mrs. Margaret Oliphant, 139[6, 7]
Ouida (Madame Ramée), 142[22], 143[32]

153

Index

Paget, Lady, 88
Pakenham, Compton T., 140[7], 149[21]
Palgrave, William Gifford, 5, 41
Pall Mall Gazette, 33-4
Palmer, Edward Henry, 138[2]
Payne, John, 2
Penzer, Norman M., 139[3]
Pitts, Joseph, 13
Pizzaro, Francisco, 83
Pope, Alexander, 48
Porter, Father, 66

Reeve, Henry, 36
Reinehr, Sister Mary Joan, 147[30]
Renan, Ernest, 45, 100
Rhodes, Cecil, 147[30]
Rousseau, 70-1
Royal Geographical Society, 8, 17
Ruskin, John, 1

Salisbury, Marquis of, Robert Cecil, 58
Saturday Review, 33, 35-6
Scaliger, Joseph, 98
Schneider, Herbert W., 139[8, 9]
Scott, Dr. Jonathan, 2
Shaw, George Bernard, 65
Smith, Byron Porter, 138[1]
Smith, Sidney, 83
Speke, Captain John Henning, 5, 8
Spencer, Herbert, 59, 63, 67
Spenser, Edmund, 100, 102
Sprenger, Alois, 99, 100
Stanley, Henry, Lord of Alderley, 64
Stead, William T., 33-4
Stisted, Georgiana, 143[32]

Strachey, Lytton, 4, 139[8]
Symons, Arthur, 143[35], 143-4[36], 144[39]

Taylor, Walt: 149-50[28], 150[29]
Thompson, Francis, 92
Tolstoy, Leo, 90
Torrens, Henry, 2
Toye, Francis, 147[30]
Treneer, Anne, 18-19, 22, 41, 100, 102, 109, 113-14, 117, 129, 140[6], 147[1], 148[15], 149[19, 22, 23, 26], 150[29]
Trevelyan, George Macaulay, 138[3]
Tryell, Father, 64, 68

Usedom, Count, 72

Vere, Aubrey de, 146[12]

Walters, Catherine ('Skittles'), 57, 69-70, 73, 85, 93
Warburton, Eliot, 5
Warner, Philip Lee, 148[13]
Watts, George Frederick, 89
Wilkins, William Henry, 142[24, 25], 143[32]
Wilkinson, Sir Gardner, 32
Wilson, Andrew, 144[40]
Windsor, Lady, 88
Wotton, Sir Henry, 114
Wright, Thomas, 53, 143[32]
Wright, William, 2, 138[2]
Wyndham, Mrs. Madeline, 57, 69

Yeats, William B., 59

For Product Safety Concerns and Information please contact our EU
representative GPSR@taylorandfrancis.com
Taylor & Francis Verlag GmbH, Kaufingerstraße 24, 80331 München, Germany

www.ingramcontent.com/pod-product-compliance
Lightning Source LLC
Chambersburg PA
CBHW052126300426
44116CB00010B/1805